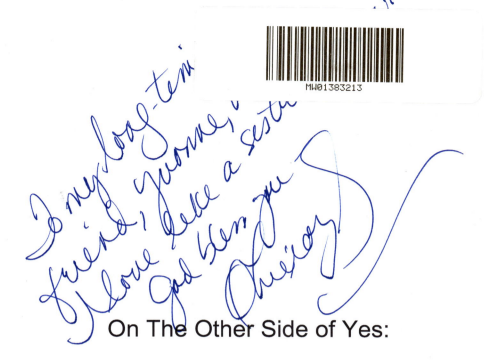

On The Other Side of Yes:

Understanding the Power of Agreement

Obieray Rogers

Forward by
Bishop Timothy J. Clarke

On the Other Side of Yes: Understanding the Power of Agreement.
Copyright © 2005 by Obieray Rogers

Scripture references noted "KJV" are taken from the Holy Bible, King James Version. Public domain.

Scripture references noted "NASB" are taken from the New American Standard Bible® Copyright©1960, 1962, 1963, 1968, 1971, 1972, 1973, 1975, 1977, 1995 by The Lockman Foundation. Used by permission. All rights reserved.

Scripture references noted "NIV" are taken from the Holy Bible, New International Version, copyright © 1973, 1978, 1984 by International Bible Society. Used by permission of Zondervan Bible Publishers. All rights reserved.

Scripture references noted "NKJV" are taken from the Holy Bible, New King James Version, copyright © 1982 by Thomas Nelson, Inc. Used by permission. All rights reserved.

Scripture references noted "NLT" are taken from the Holy Bible, New Living Translation, copyright © 1996. Used by permission of Tyndale House Publishers, Inc., Wheaton, Illinois 60189. All rights reserved.

Scripture references noted "NRSV" are taken from the Holy Bible, New Revised Standard Version, copyright 1989, Division of Christian Education of the National Council of the Churches of Christ in the United States of America. Used by permission. All rights reserved.

Scriptures references noted "The Message" are taken from *The Message.* Copyright © 1993, 1994, 1995, 1996, 2000, 2001, 2002. Used by permission of NavPress Publishing Group. All rights reserved.

All rights reserved. No part of this publication may be reproduced, stored in a retrieval system, or transmitted in any form or by any means electronic, mechanical, photocopy, recording or otherwise except for brief extracts for the purpose of review, without the prior permission of the publisher and copyright owner.

ISBN 978-14664224-2-1

Printed in the United States of America

For Diann and Ivan

Acknowledgments

I thank God that He continues to use me to write and constantly reveals ideas for potential books to me. He is the true author of everything I write; I am well aware that without Him I can do nothing.

I thank God for my Bishop and First Lady—Timothy and Clytemnestra Clarke—who have provided spiritual covering for me throughout the years. I am grateful that God saw fit to put me under their ministry.

I thank God for my family and friends who support and encourage the work that I do. I especially want to thank my oldest sister, Diann, who provided great feedback which led to some interesting discussions. I also want to acknowledge my youngest brother, Ivan, who passed away in 2010. He and I shared a love of reading and spent quite a bit of time comparing and discussing books. He was one of my biggest fans and was always telling his friends that they needed to buy his sister's books! He was a good friend, as well as a brother, and he will be forever missed.

I thank God for my critique group—Rita and Tamika Braswell, Michael Flemmings, Dwayne Manning, Diann Jones-Adams—and my editor—Yvonne Cobb—who all provided invaluable feedback. They were a blessing to me.

And, finally, I thank God for you. I pray as I write that whoever reads my work will be blessed, and I trust that my prayer was answered. Thank you.

Foreword

One of the ways that I determine the value of something, especially a book or a sermon, is based on what I call its "portability." By that I mean my ability to transport it, use it and implement it right away; in other words, does it work?

Based on my informal test, the book you are reading is indeed a valuable one. The reason I say that is because on the day after I read the "galley" copy of this book, I was quoting it in a meeting with my staff. That is what I call, "portability"

The principal that Obie Rogers lifts up in *On the Other Side of Yes: Understanding the Power of Agreement* is one of the ancient and proven truths that work and succeed time and time again. One of the clearest pictures of this is the biblical story of the tower of Babel. In that story God says of those seeking to build a tower to heaven, *"Look, they are one people, and they have all one language; and this is only the beginning of what they will do; nothing that they propose to do will now be impossible for them"* (Genesis 11:6, NRSV). Why did God say that? Because even though their intentions were wrong, the people had tapped into the power of agreement.

Agreement is necessary in a marriage, in a family, in a business partnership, even in a friendship and as Ms. Rogers points out, when we tap into it, we become almost unstoppable.

Agreement is never easy to achieve, which is why so many choose or opt to just get along or even worse, go along, but when we are willing to do the hard spade work of agreement, what results is well worth the effort and energy to reach it.

I pray that God will sink the truths of this book and the principal it explores to become not just part of your lexicon, but of your life as well. Read it and be blessed. Read it and be changed.

Bishop Timothy J. Clarke
Senior Pastor
First Church of God, Columbus, OH

Table of Contents

Introduction 1

PART ONE

Chapter One — 9

Hey, Can You Do Me A Favor? ....

Chapter Two — 19

What Have I Gotten Myself Into? ....

PART TWO

Chapter Three — 31

Liar, Liar, Pants On Fire! ....

Chapter Four — 43

The Professor Is In ....

Chapter Five — 53

Wait! You Haven't Heard The Whole Story Yet ....

Chapter Six — 65

Sisters On A Mission ....

Chapter Seven — 75

So Much To Do, So Little Time ....

Chapter Eight — 85

Let's Give A Shout Out To Forest Gump ....

Chapter Nine — 93

Evil, Eviler, Evilest ....

Chapter Ten — 101
Clicking Your Heels Three Times And Wishing For Home
Only Works In The Movies ....

Chapter Eleven — 107
What? Don't Tell Me You Didn't Know That Was Going to
Happen ....

Chapter Twelve — 113
Ain't You Got No Home Trainin'? ....

Chapter Thirteen — 121
Can I Get A Witness? ....

PART THREE

Chapter Fourteen — 135
Don't You Want To Know How I Really Feel? ....
Conclusion 151

Introduction

Have you ever read something that kept you thinking about the subject long after you finished? Something that was so enlightening that it caused you to examine your thinking or behavior? It doesn't happen often, but when it does, all you can say is, "Wow!"

I had often heard, and had even quoted, Amos 3:3 (KJV), *"Can two walk together, except they be agreed,"* but it wasn't until I read a magazine article in my doctor's waiting room that I understood what the Scripture meant. I don't remember the name of the magazine or who wrote the article; I just remember the content: Entering into agreement with someone of the same mindset will manifest itself in a powerful way.

I must admit that prior to reading the magazine article I never gave a lot of thought to what I agreed to or who I was agreeing with. If someone asked me to do something that I wanted to do, I did it; if not, I didn't. It was no big deal and, thankfully, I never willingly agreed to anything crazy, illegal or dishonest.

The article I am referring to was written by a married couple chronicling the story of their son who was born with a congenital illness. The doctors advised the parents to terminate the pregnancy. They listened to the doctor's reasoning for termination, and after extensive prayer, decided to have the baby. The parents didn't know everything the child would face, but knew that whatever was ahead would be demanding and involve long hospital stays and multiple operations; they chose to proceed in faith. The parents committed to be in total agreement about their child's treatment before he was born, and were at peace because they agreed they were doing what they believed to be best.

Once the child was born he did face daunting physical challenges. Despite all of that, the parents were always in agreement about their child's treatment, even when it went against the doctors' recommendations. That is not to say that they didn't esteem the doctors, because they had confidence in their training; however, it is to say that this couple had their faith in the Great Physician, and every step of the way they were seeking God for guidance.

Their family and friends certainly may not have understood the why of their decisions, and perhaps you can't either, but the fact that they were in agreement was the remarkable thing to me. Their son's eventual death didn't pull them apart, but drew them closer because they had agreed to celebrate every day of their child's life.

One of the most amazing things to me about the article was that by agreeing to agree this couple prevented the devil from gaining a toe-hold into their relationship. They effectively diffused the spirit of blame that frequently occurs when something happens. You know the if-you-had-done-this-then-I-would-have-done-that game that so often complicates our relationships, especially when something unpleasant happens.

After reading the article, I began to reevaluate my own views and study how important and powerful agreement actually is. I had an opportunity to present a workshop on this subject at the Chicagoland (Illinois) Sunday School Association conference as an elective course a few years ago, but with only one hour to present I wasn't able to get into the subject the way I wanted. But I became fascinated with the subject of agreement. This book is a result of my research, and I have discovered three essential truths:

- You can agree with yourself: Will you eat another piece of cake or go for a walk? Will you spend your last dollar to play the lottery or save it toward paying your bills? Will you spend more time in the Word or continue wasting time doing other things that are less important?

Introduction

- You can agree with someone else: Will you loan someone money until pay day or will you participate in an armed bank robbery? Will you go to Bible study or to happy hour with your friends?
- You can agree with God: This one is a little more challenging, because if things don't work out the way you want—unlike agreeing with yourself or someone else where you can blame someone or some thing if things don't work out—you can't blame God. He is perfect, which means that whatever you agreed with Him to do is perfect, too. You have to accept the outcome and believe that things worked out the way they were supposed to, even if you don't like the way they worked out.

A MARRIAGE MADE IN HEAVEN

The greatest tool in the Christian's arsenal is the power of the Holy Spirit and all that He brings with Him when we say yes to His coming into our lives. Sometimes we take for granted just how much power the Holy Spirit endows us with when we accept Jesus Christ as our Lord and Savior. The Bible tells us that, *"The tongue has the power of life and death"* (Proverbs 18:21, NIV), and we know that we should, *"Simply let your 'Yes' be 'Yes,', and your 'No' be 'No'"* (Matthew 5:37, NIV), but I often wonder if we really understand just how much power we have when two or more of us come into agreement:

> *Take this most seriously: A yes on earth is a yes in heaven; a no on earth is no in heaven. What you say to one another is eternal. I mean this. When two of you get together on anything at all on earth and make a prayer of it, my Father in heaven goes into action. And when two or three of you are together be-*

3

cause of me, you can be sure that I'll be there
(Matthew 18:19, The Message).

The importance of intercessory prayer cannot be minimized, and one of the best places to practice the power of agreement is during corporate worship. There is not a person saved today who hasn't benefited from someone standing in the gap for them. We need to agree with the intercessor, whether we like their style of praying or not. Some intercessors are very loud (almost as if they believe God is deaf) while others are very soft-spoken. Yet, all have the ability to touch heaven, and so do we when we line up in agreement with them. When my pastor prays after the intercessor, he sometimes says one of two phrases: "We agree with the foregone prayer" or "We agree with everything the man (or woman) of God just prayed," because he understands the results that come from agreeing with a like-minded person.

We can also practice the power of agreement during the sermon. The man or woman of God who is bringing forth the Word has already studied and prepared. We can make their delivery easier by agreeing with them before, during and after the preaching.

A final place to practice agreement is during the altar call. Can you imagine what would happen if every believer got into agreement with what God does during the altar call? That is not the time for you to tip out so you can beat the traffic or take a potty break. Lives and souls are at stake, and one day it may be your family member fighting for domination of their soul. What would you prefer: Someone agreeing with the man or woman of God or someone who just had to leave for no reason other than not wanting to sit in line to get out of the parking lot?

SO WHAT'S THE BIG DEAL ABOUT AGREEMENT?

On the Other Side of Yes: Understanding the Power of Agreement contains what I believe to be the ideal biblical

Introduction

illustrations of diverse types of agreements. Regardless of whether you are in complete accord, or involved in an agreement because of someone else's decision, there is no turning back once a "yes" response has been given.

The big deal about agreements is that they are powerful and permanent. You can't undo the events that are set in motion, whether good or bad, when you join in agreement. And, because they are so powerful and permanent, you must be careful about the agreements you make.

By the end of this book you will have discovered that agreements can be positive and negative, potent and dangerous, rewarding and fulfilling. You will be reminded that who you agree with is just as important as what you are agreeing on, and that whether you agree by saying yes, okay, uh-huh, nodding your head, grunting, moaning or remaining silent, the principle of Amos 3:3 remains the same: *"Can two walk together, except they be agreed?"*

PART ONE

DON'T JUMP IN THE POOL BEFORE YOU CHECK FOR WATER

Clarification: To be free of confusion.

Chapter One —
Hey, Can You Do Me A Favor?

One of my favorite television game shows is *The Family Feud*. I like watching the teams match wits, and enjoy talking back to my television when someone gives a really bad answer or laughing out loud when they give a funny one. I have noticed that some of the contestants are more competitive than others and try to buzz in to answer the initial question before the host gets a chance to finish asking it. Sometimes the strategy works, but more often than not it backfires, because once the question is fully read the answer given makes no sense. For example someone will answer, "Baseball" when what the host was going to read was, "We surveyed one hundred people and asked them to name a round, red vegetable that is really a fruit." (The answer is a tomato, which as you can see clearly has nothing to do with baseball).

Some of us do the same thing when entering into agreements with our family, friends and acquaintances. A "yes" response sets in motion actions that cannot always be changed or stopped regardless of whether the agreement is for spiritual, physical, emotional or financial reasons. My goal is to give you enough information to make an informed decision the next time someone says, "Hey, can you do me a favor?"

THE ANATOMY OF AN AGREEMENT

When some people are asked to do a favor their immediate response is, "Sure," without even knowing what you want. Others might respond with a tentative, "Maybe," while waiting for more information. But a wise person will wait to get as much information as possible before making a decision to avoid ending up in an unpleasant situation: "Tell me what you need and I will let you know if I can help." I am not suggesting that you don't help people; all I am suggesting is that perhaps you might want to find out exactly what is involved before you get into something you might regret.

The following are the six primary issues I believe must be clarified before entering into any type of agreement:

YOU MUST BE WILLING TO ACCEPT THE CONDITIONS OF THE AGREEMENT

Agreement always involves an element of obedience. I had a former boss who always said, "If you haven't done it all, you haven't done it at all," and every time I heard it I wanted to cringe. Partly because she was right and partly because it reminded me that doing something halfway is never acceptable.

Israel's first king, Saul, had been told to destroy the Amalekites because they had attacked the children of Israel at Rephidim (Exodus 17:8-16). God's instructions were very clear: Saul was to kill everything and everybody. For reasons known only to him, Saul chose to spare King Agag's life as well as keep the best of the animals for himself. God sent Samuel to confront Saul about his actions:

> *"When you started out in this, you were nothing—and you knew it. Then God put you at the head of Israel—made you king over Israel. Then God sent you off to do a job for him, ordering you, 'Go and put those sinners, the Amalekites, under a holy ban. Go to war against them until you have totally wiped them out.' So why did you not obey God? Why did you grab all this loot? Why, with God's eyes on you all the time, did you brazenly carry out this evil?" Saul defended himself. "What are you talking about? I did obey God. I did the job God set for me. I brought in*

Chapter One — Hey, Can You Do Me A Favor?

*King Agag and destroyed the Amalekites un-
der the terms of the holy ban. So the soldiers
saved back a few choice sheep and cattle
from the holy ban for sacrifice to God at Gil-
gal—what's wrong with that?"* (I Samuel
15:17-21, The Message).

Saul's inability to understand that partial obedience is
actually disobedience caused him to lose his kingdom. His
offer of repentance was too little, too late: *"You rejected
God's command. Now God has rejected you as king over
Israel"* (I Samuel 15:26, The Message).

You may not have a kingdom to lose like Saul, but
there is still a lot to be learned from his example.

YOU MUST BE OBEDIENT TO THE INSTRUCTIONS

Before his conversion and name change, Saul was on fire
against Christ's disciples. He had received permission and
arrest warrants from the Chief Priest to bring any disciples
he found to Jerusalem to trial. While on the road to Damascus, Saul saw an intense light that knocked him to the
ground and he heard a voice say, *"Saul, Saul, why are you
out to get me?"* He inquired as to who was speaking and was
told, *"I am Jesus, the One you're hunting down. I want you
to get up and enter the city. In the city you'll be told what to
do next,"* (Acts 9:1-6, The Message). When Saul got up from
the ground he discovered that although he could open his
eyes, he was blind. The men who were with him lead him
into Damascus. For three days, he couldn't see and he
didn't have anything to eat or drink. During that time he
had a vision showing a man by the name of Ananias restor-
ing his sight. Meanwhile Ananias was having a similar
encounter:

*"Get up and go over to Straight Avenue. Ask
at the house of Judas for a man from Tarsus.*

11

His name is Saul. He's there praying. He has just had a dream in which he saw a man named Ananias enter the house and lay hands on him so he could see again." Ananias protested, "Master, you can't be serious. Everybody's talking about this man and the terrible things he's been doing, his reign of terror against your people in Jerusalem! And now he's shown up here with papers from the Chief Priest that give him license to do the same to us." But the Master said, "Don't argue. Go! I have picked him as my personal representative to Gentiles and kings and Jews. And now I'm about to show him what he's in for—the hard suffering that goes with this job" (Acts 9:10-16, The Message).

Ananias did as the Lord requested. When he laid his hands on Saul, scales fell from Saul's eyes and he was able to see. Once Saul's sight was restored he was baptized, got something to eat and proceeded to fulfill his true purpose in life.

YOU MUST BE COMMITTED TO SEEING THE AGREEMENT THROUGH TO THE END

Have you ever started something and then wanted to stop in the middle of it because you realized it was going to be harder than you thought?

The Bible shares the sad and distressing story of two desperate mothers who devised a most unusual agreement to get them through a famine. The problem with a famine—other than the obvious of there not being enough food—is that you are not sure when it is going to end. Since you don't know when the famine will end, you also don't know what to do. Do you wait another day and hope that is the day of deliverance? Or do you assume that since the famine has gone on this long, it will probably continue. It is a

Chapter One — Hey, Can You Do Me A Favor?

dangerous position to be in when you have lost hope and you are unable to see, and no longer expect, that relief is going to come:

> *One day the king of Israel was walking along the city wall. A woman cried out, "Help! Your majesty!"…She said, "This woman came to me and said, 'Give up your son and we'll have him for today's supper; tomorrow we'll eat my son.' So we cooked my son and ate him. The next day I told her, 'Your turn—bring your son so we can have him for supper.' But she had hidden her son away"* (2 Kings, 6:24, 25(a), 26-29, The Message).

I am sure that once the first mother had gotten over the obscene repulsion of the suggestion, and then the actual implementation of the act of killing and eating her child, that the last thing she expected was that the other mother wouldn't keep her part of the agreement. Regardless of the reason for hiding her son away, both the king and the first mother were helpless to do anything about the situation. They couldn't undo what had already been done.

YOU MUST HAVE FAITH TO BELIEVE THAT WHAT YOU WANT TO HAPPEN IS GOING TO HAPPEN

The book of Acts tells us that King Herod Agrippa went on a rampage and arrested people who belonged to the church. He had John's brother, James, killed and figured that since that made some of the Jews happy, he would go after Peter. He had him arrested and jailed during the Feast of Unleavened Bread with a court date scheduled for immediately after the feast. When the Church heard about Peter's arrest they began to pray:

Then the time came for Herod to bring him out for the kill. That night, even though shackled to two soldiers, one on either side, Peter slept like a baby. And there were guards at the door keeping their eyes on the place. Herod was taking no chances! Suddenly there was an angel at his side and light flooding the room. The angel shook Peter and got him up: "Hurry!" The handcuffs fell off his wrists. The angel said, "Get dressed. Put on your shoes." Peter did it. Then, "Grab your coat and let's get out of here." Peter followed him, but didn't believe it was really an angel—he thought he was dreaming (Acts 12:6-9, The Message).

Once Peter realized he wasn't dreaming, he went to the house where the Church had gathered to pray. He knocked on the door; a servant girl answered, recognized Peter's voice, left him standing at the gate and ran back to tell the others he was there. And you know what? After all that praying and seeking God for help, the Church didn't believe her! But Peter kept knocking until they finally let him in (Acts 12:12-16).

YOU MUST BE WILLING TO REAP THE REWARDS OR ACCEPT THE CONSEQUENCES

I recently read an article where actress Tyne Daly was being interviewed about her latest role portraying Maria Callas, the legendary opera diva. Ms. Daly made a statement while speaking in reference to her illustrious career that I thought was pretty enlightening: "You can get flattered into a lot of bad situations in this business."

The apostle Paul would probably agree with Ms. Daly, because he knew better than to let people flatter him into stepping outside of God's will and doing his own thing. Whenever God uses us in an unusual or mighty way, there

Chapter One — Hey, Can You Do Me A Favor?

is a tendency to let our egos run amok. What prevents this from happening is our being securely rooted and grounded in the knowledge that without God we can do nothing. People will pump you up, and if you are not careful you will start believing what they say instead of staying true to what God has called you to do.

There is no denying that Paul was anointed to do a lot of things; among them was the ability to cast out demons. Sadly there were seven men who didn't fully understand how the anointing worked. They thought the anointing was manufactured and that anyone could do miracles. They found out the hard way the faultiness of their logic:

> *God did powerful things through Paul, things quite out of the ordinary. The word got around and people started taking pieces of clothing—handkerchiefs and scarves and the like—that had touched Paul's skin and then touching the sick with them. The touch did it—they were healed and whole. Some itinerant Jewish exorcists who happened to be in town at the time tried their hand at what they assumed to be Paul's "game." They pronounced the name of the Master Jesus over victims of evil spirits, saying, "I command you by the Jesus preached by Paul!" The seven sons of a certain Sceva, a Jewish high priest, were trying to do this on a man when the evil spirit talked back: "I know Jesus and I've heard of Paul but who are you?" Then the possessed man went berserk—jumped the exorcists, beat them up, and tore off their clothes. Naked and bloody, they got away as best they could* (Acts 19:11-16, The Message).

While the anointing can be transferred (such as in the case of Elijah and Elisha), this was undoubtedly not God's plan

15

for these men. They probably didn't even believe in Jesus and only wanted the fame and attention they saw Paul receiving. Well, as the saying goes, you should be careful what you ask for. They did receive fame when news of their humiliation spread all over Ephesus among both the Jews and Greeks. The good news about the gossip was that it created a reverence for God and caused a lifestyle change: *"Many of those who thus believed came out of the closet and made a clean break with their secret sorceries"* (Acts 19:18, The Message).

YOU MUST FOCUS ON THE END RESULT AND KEEP THE GOAL IN MIND

The greatest example of this is Jesus Christ. He knew before He took on the form of a human and completed His mission on earth, that His journey would be filled with people who would embrace and believe everything about Him, as well as those that wouldn't:

> *When it came close to the time for His Ascension, He gathered up His courage and steeled Himself for the journey to Jerusalem. He sent messengers on ahead. They came to a Samaritan village to make arrangements for His hospitality. But when the Samaritans learned that His destination was Jerusalem, they refused hospitality. When the disciples James and John learned of it, they said, "Master, do you want us to call a bolt of lightning down out of the sky and incinerate them?" Jesus turned on them: "Of course not!" And they traveled on to another village* (Luke 9:51-56, The Message).

In the face of the horrible death that awaited Him, Jesus chose to focus on the end result: The salvation of His

Chapter One — Hey, Can You Do Me A Favor?

people. Now I don't know about you, but that is the best news I have ever heard. Hallelujah

Chapter Two — What Have I Gotten Myself Into?

Have you ever agreed to do something and then wondered what exactly were you thinking about when you said yes? This usually happens when what appears to be a simple request morphs into a gigantic pain in the neck.

I am employed by the City of Columbus (Ohio). The division I work in is responsible for maintaining close to five million square feet of city-owned property to include everything from changing a light bulb to constructing a new building. No matter what the request is, at some point people are going to talk with me. My unofficial title is Peacekeeper, but my primary job is to act as a liaison between those who need work done, those who do the work and to direct people to the appropriate contact person if the request is something my division doesn't handle. I have a good relationship with my co-workers and whenever I have to ask for a favor I usually get a good response.

Recently one of our clients needed to have something done in her office and waited until the last minute to put in her request so, of course, you know the work needed to be done immediately! She had e-mailed in her request and then followed up with a phone call to stress the urgency of having the work done the same day. I told her the men were swamped, but that I would see what I could do. I talked to one of the supervisors, explained the situation the way it had been explained to me and he was willing to readjust the schedule to do this *favor*. I am emphazing the word favor because when the men got to the client's office, they discovered that the job involved a lot more than what was told to us, but they were willing to go ahead and take care of everything the client needed.

The client called while the men were still there to express her appreciation for a quick turnaround. Then before she got off the phone she said, "Oh, yeah, by the way, one of my co-workers was wondering if the guys could move something in her office since they're already here." Because it was simply moving an empty file cabinet from one wall to another, which would take all of two minutes, permission was granted. A few minutes later the co-worker with the file cabinet called to thank me for getting the move done, and one of her co-workers got on the phone to request that we rearrange her entire office that day! Can you believe it? I told her that she would have to put in a written request and the move would be put on the calendar. After talking to these three women I concluded that some people know how to take the "give an inch, take a mile" philosophy to an entirely different level.

Let's examine some more aspects of an agreement based on definitions provided by Webster's Collegiate Dictionary, tenth edition.

AGREEMENT IMPLIES COMPLETE ACCORD USUALLY ATTAINED BY DISCUSSION AND THEN AN ADJUSTMENT OF DIFFERENCES

This section title sounds like a mouthful, doesn't it? But, I believe a good example of this is the ministerial team of Paul and Barnabas. When Paul and Barnabas were commissioned in Acts chapter thirteen to go on their first missionary trip, they took John Mark with them as an assistant. He stayed with them as far as Pamphylla and then decided to go back to Jerusalem (Acts 13:13). Paul and Barnabas continued on with their mission of planting churches, and it is not until we get to Acts chapter fifteen that we find out how Paul really felt about John Mark's leaving.

Paul wanted to go on a second missionary trip to check on the churches they had planted. Barnabas agreed, but he wanted to take John Mark with them; Paul was against the idea because John Mark had left in the middle of the first trip. Barnabas wanted to give him another

Chapter Two — What Have I Gotten Myself Into?

chance; Paul said no and that is when the discussions began. We can only imagine that they were heated—the NIV version of Acts 15:39 refers to it as a sharp disagreement—which is usually what happens when you get two passionate people together. Because they were unable to reconcile their differences, they agreed to end the partnership.

There are biblical commentators who believe that Barnabas was wrong for leaving. They base their conjecture on the fact that Paul went on to become one of the better known apostles and is credited with writing a good portion of the New Testament, whereas you hear very little about Barnabas after the book of Acts. There may be some validity to that, but I don't for a moment believe Barnabas' decision was an easy one. Paul and Barnabas had spent years working together, and there was a bond between them that couldn't be easily broken:

> *When he came to Jerusalem, he tried to join the disciples, but they were all afraid of him, not believing that he really was a disciple. But Barnabas took him and brought him to the apostles. He told them how Saul on his journey had seen the Lord and that the Lord had spoken to him, and how in Damascus he had preached fearlessly in the name of Jesus* (Acts 9:26-27, NIV).

Acts 11:25-26 tells us that Barnabas was the one who brought Paul to Antioch where they would eventually spend a year together in ministry before their first missionary journey:

> *Then Barnabas went to Tarsus to look for Saul, and when he found him, he brought him to Antioch. So for a whole year Barnabas and Saul met with the church and taught great numbers of people. The disciples were called*

21

Christians first at Antioch (Acts 11:25-26, NIV).

I believe Barnabas reluctantly agreed to end the partnership only after spending time in prayer, fasting and allowing the Holy Spirit to lead him. Their separation didn't destroy their personal relationship, only their ministerial partnership. Barnabas had been too much of an integral part of Paul's life when he was most impressionable. He was a teacher and mentor to him in his early Christian walk, and Paul didn't forget him. (Don't you still think of the people who helped you when you were in a spiritually vulnerable or immature state?). Barnabas, like others who realize they are merely an instrument to be used by God, knew that his assignment with Paul was finished.

In the end it was decided that they would agree to disagree and they parted ways: Barnabas took his cousin, John Mark, and sailed for Cyprus, where under his tutelage John Mark developed spiritual maturity. Paul began working with Silas and headed for Syria and Cilicia. Eventually Paul did agree to give John Mark another chance as evidenced by Colossians 4:10: *"My fellow prisoner Aristarchus sends you his greetings, as does Mark, the cousin of Barnabas. (You have received instructions about him; if he comes to you, welcome him)"* and 2 Timothy 4:11, *"...Get Mark and bring him with you, because he is helpful to me in my ministry."* Although their spiritual partnership had ended, Paul and Barnabas continued to do the work of the Lord in their own unique way and maintained fond memories of each other.

Everybody needs a Barnabas in their life. Someone who will be loyal, faithful and dependable enough to stand up for what they believe to be right, even if the decision results in a separation.

Chapter Two — What Have I Gotten Myself Into?

AGREEMENT IMPLIES A HARMONY OF OPINION, ACTION OR CHARACTER

As previously stated, Paul and Barnabas had just parted ways because of their disagreement regarding John Mark. Paul chose Silas as his partner for his second missionary trip, and they were, *"...commended by the brothers to the grace of the Lord to continue their missionary work"* (Acts 15:40, NIV). While ministering in Philippi, they were constantly harassed by a young girl who enjoyed shouting, *"These men are servants of the Most High God, who are telling you the way to be saved"* (Acts 16:17, NIV). After several days of this Paul had had enough and rebuked the evil spirit in the girl: *"In the name of Jesus Christ I command you to come out of her!"* (Acts 16:18, NIV). The spirit left the girl and her owners were angry because their source of income had dried up. They had Paul and Silas arrested, beaten and thrown in jail.

Jails in those days were not like the ones you see depicted in movies and on television. Prisoners were attached to the wall with their arms and legs chained. It was a very uncomfortable position to be in and probably made sleep virtually impossible. Take a note here: Sometimes entering into an agreement causes unforeseen events and circumstances that are out of our control. Paul was the one who rebuked the evil spirit, yet he and Silas were beaten and thrown into jail.

One sleepless night while pondering the goodness of God, Paul began to worship and praise. And instead of Silas having an attitude and thinking, *He's got a lot of nerve making all that noise. This is his fault! If he had just kept his big mouth shut and let that girl alone, I wouldn't be here shackled in a cold, damp prison. Now he's singing loud—and off key—and all I want to do is get some sleep!* the Bible lets us know that both Paul and Silas took advantage of their predicament and their captive audience:

23

Obieray Rogers

About midnight Paul and Silas were praying and singing hymns to God, and other prisoners were listening to them. Suddenly there was such a violent earthquake that the foundations of the prison were shaken. At once all the prison doors flew open, and everybody's chains came loose. The jailer woke up, and when he saw the prison doors open, he drew his sword and was about to kill himself because he thought the prisoners had escaped. But Paul shouted, "Don't harm yourself! We are all here!" The jailer called for lights, rushed in and fell trembling before Paul and Silas. He then brought them out and asked, "Sirs, what must I do to be saved?" (Acts 16:25-30, NIV).

Paul and Silas shared the Word of the Lord with him, and the jailer and his entire household were saved. The jailer took Paul and Silas to his home, washed their wounds and fed them. In the morning, word was sent to the jailer to release the prisoners, but Paul and Silas refused to go quietly:

But Paul said to the officers: they beat us publicly without a trial, even though we are Roman citizens, and threw us into prison. And now do they want to get rid of us quietly? No! Let them come themselves and escort us out...When they heard that Paul and Silas were Roman citizens, they were alarmed. They came to appease them and escorted them from the prison, requesting them to leave the city. After Paul and Silas came out of the prison, they went to Lydia's house, where they met with the brothers and en-

Chapter Two — What Have I Gotten Myself Into?

couraged them. Then they left (Acts 16:37-40, NIV).

Paul and Silas were in harmony about their actions. They had agreed to be a ministerial team, and their love for the Lord, and each other, was more important than any physical inconveniences they had to endure.

AGREEMENT IMPLIES A WILLINGNESS TO ACCEPT OR CONCEDE SOMETHING (AS TO THE VIEWS OR WISHES OF ANOTHER)

Esther was a young Jewish woman who was raised by her cousin Mordecai as his own daughter because both of her parents were deceased. When King Xerxes banished Queen Vashti from the palace, he went on a quest to find a new queen. All of the beautiful young virgins were brought before the king's men for inspection; those who received approval were taken to the palace where they would undergo beauty treatments and be given an opportunity to please the king. The one whom the king found most favorable would become queen. Because Esther was lovely in form and features, she found favor with King Xerxes and became the queen (Esther 2:1-17). However, before any of this process began Mordecai forbade Esther from revealing her nationality; no one in the palace was aware that she was Jewish.

Mordecai regularly went to the palace gate to check on Esther and while there overheard a plot to assassinate the king. He told Esther; she told the king and the culprits were caught and executed (Esther 2:21-23).

In the meantime the king had promoted one of his men, Haman, to Prime Minister, putting him directly under the king in terms of power. Royal officials knelt down and paid honor to him, but Mordecai refused to bow down or show respect:

> *When Haman saw that Mordecai would not kneel down or pay him honor, he was enraged. Yet having learned who Mordecai's people were, he scorned the idea of killing only Mordecai. Instead Haman looked for a way to destroy all of Mordecai's people, the Jews, throughout the whole kingdom of Xerxes* (Esther 3:5-6, NIV).

Haman convinced the king to sign a decree to destroy the Jews. When Mordecai heard of it, he tore his clothes as a sign of grief, put on sackcloth and ashes, and wailed loudly and bitterly in the city. He stopped at the king's gate and stayed there. When word came to Esther about what he was doing, she sent a servant to inquire as to why. Mordecai sent word back and urged her to seek an audience with the king. Esther responded that an audience with the king was by invitation only, and to go uninvited could possibly result in death. While Esther's reluctance was reasonable and perhaps even understandable, Mordecai's response was clear as to what he expected:

> *Do not think that because you are in the king's house you alone of all the Jews will escape. For if you remain silent at this time, relief and deliverance for the Jews will arise from another place, but you and your father's family will perish. And who knows but that you have come to royal position for such a time as this?* (Esther 4:13-14, NIV).

Esther agreed to what Mordecai asked and requested that all of the Jews in Susa fast for her by not eating or drinking for three days; she and her maids would do the same. At the end of the fast, she would go into the king. When the fast ended, Esther did approach the king and he invited her in by holding out his scepter. He asked her what she wanted

Chapter Two — What Have I Gotten Myself Into?

and offered to give her anything, up to and including half of his kingdom. She asked for a banquet to be held with the king and Haman in attendance. The king granted her request and plans were made.

When Haman heard that he would be the only invited guest at a banquet with the king and queen, he rushed home to share the good news with his wife and family. Before he left the palace grounds he encountered Mordecai who again refused to bow down to him. Haman allowed his anger at the slight to put a damper on his excitement. He told his wife and family about Mordecai, and their solution was for him to construct a seventy-five foot gallow and have Mordecai hung (Esther 5:9-14).

At the banquet the king asked Esther to tell him what she wanted and again told her he would give her anything, up to and including half of his kingdom. Esther's request was to have a second banquet the following night with Haman in attendance. The king granted her request.

That night the king had insomnia and ordered that the book of the chronicles be read to him. He discovered the role Mordecai had played in the failed assassination attempt against him, and was dismayed to realize that nothing had been done for Mordecai as a reward for his loyalty. The next morning he asked Haman what should be done for, "the man the king delights to honor," and Haman went through a list of elaborate things that would befit such a man, because in his arrogance he assumed the king was talking about him. What profound humiliation Haman must have felt when he discovered that the king was speaking of Mordecai and then ordered him to fulfill all of the elaborate plans he had just shared (Esther 6:6-11).

Upon arrival for the second night of the banquet feast, the king asked Esther for the third time what she wanted, and once again offered up to half of his kingdom. Her response was a plea for her life and the life of her people:

27

> *"...For I and my people have been sold for de-*
> *struction and slaughter and annihilation. If*
> *we had merely been sold as male and female*
> *slaves, I would have kept quiet, because no*
> *such distress would justify disturbing the*
> *king." King Xerxes asked Queen Esther, "Who*
> *is he? Where is the man who has dared to do*
> *such a thing?" Esther said, "The adversary*
> *and enemy is this vile Haman"* (Esther 7:3-6,
> NIV).

The story ends with the Jewish people being saved, and Haman being hung on the gallows he had constructed for Mordecai.

All of the biblical characters mentioned in this chapter at one point probably wondered what had they gotten themselves into. Their obedience to God caused some of them to be put in precarious positions. But, the reality is that only God knows what is ahead and we have to trust that He knows what He is doing and where and how He is leading us. Entering into an agreement with God will always turn out right.

PART TWO

CONGRATULATIONS! YOU'VE JUST BEEN ACCEPTED INTO GRADUATE SCHOOL.

Elder: One who has authority by virtue of age and experience.

Chapter Three —
Liar, Liar, Pants On Fire!

Whenever I read the intriguing Genesis account of Joseph's brothers agreeing to betray him, there is one question I can't help but ask: How could they do that to their own flesh and blood? I don't believe there is any one answer to this question; however, I do believe that there are certain family traits passed down through the years that make duplicity easy to embrace. In order to understand the brothers' betrayal you have to look at their lineage. What you will discover is a multi-generational heritage of the unlikely combination of faith and deception.

A LIE BY ANY OTHER NAME IS STILL A LIE

If you are over the age of fifty, you have probably heard the children's chant: "Liar, liar, pants on fire. Hangin' on a telephone wire," which is a loose paraphrase of the William Blake 1810 ode to dishonesty, *The Liar*. The first word of the first line is "deceiver," a word used to describe a person who leads you to believe something that is not true. As a society we tend to look down on dishonest, deceptive and untrustworthy people. Yet, society has also come to embrace the concept of the little white lie, a seemingly harmless response which may have big consequences.

- *"It's good to see you again,"* said to someone you can barely remember meeting and whose name you certainly can't recall. (You hope that they will move on before you have to admit that).
- *"Wow, this is just what I wanted,"* said to someone who has given you such a horrible gift, that you can't wait to exchange it.

- *"No, Mom, I didn't eat the last piece of cake,"* as the crumbs around your mouth and down your shirt clearly indicate otherwise.
- *"Yes, dear, you look very nice in that dress,"* a man says to a woman although the dress might not fit the way it once did.
- *"It was nice meeting you,"* said to the most boring person you have ever encountered in your life, knowing that if you see them again you will quickly go in the opposite direction.

At some point most people will give voice to an occasional white lie, but sometimes people take a seemingly harmless intent to the extreme.

MY SISTER, MY WIFE; MY WIFE, MY SISTER

The patriarch Abraham suffered from the same malady we all have: The struggle between our spiritual side and our humanity. When we allow the spiritual side to rule, we do things that are moral and upright; when our humanity gets in the way we do things like lie, steal and cheat. Abraham knew he had been called to greatness:

> *Then the Lord told Abram, "Leave your country, your relatives, and your father's house, and go to the land that I will show you. I will cause you to become the father of a great nation. I will bless you and make you famous, and I will make you a blessing to others. I will bless those who bless you and curse those who curse you. All the families of the earth will be blessed through you"* (Genesis 12:1-3, NLT).

Before Abram and his family reached the land God had for them they made a stop in Egypt. Abram decided that since

Chapter Three — Liar, Liar, Pants On Fire!

Sarai was so beautiful they should tell everyone they were brother and sister, because he knew that royalty during this time had a tendency to take what they wanted from whomever they wanted, whether it was people or possessions. While technically what Abram said was true—he and Sarai had the same father, but different mothers (Genesis 20:12)—the bottom line is that when it was convenient, Sarai was his wife; when it was inconvenient, she became his sister.

I must confess I have always resented Abram's treatment of his wife, and in a judgmental way wondered how he could be so blessed by God and still do something so stupid. But then I realized that God had counted him righteous, even knowing what he was going to do, which makes me extremely thankful that God doesn't hold imperfection against His people, including me. Having said that, I must confess I still have two major problems with Abram and Sarai's agreement to deceive unsuspecting people.

ISSUE #1—Abram treated Sarai more like a possession than a person he supposedly loved:

> *As he was approaching the border of Egypt, Abram said to his wife, Sarai, "Look, you are a very beautiful woman. When the Egyptians see you, they will say, 'This is his wife.* **Let's kill him***; then we can have her!' So please tell them you are my sister. Then they will* **spare my life** *and* **treat me well** *because of their interest in you"* (Genesis 12:11-13, NLT, emphasis mine).

Abram might not have known everything that would happen in Pharaoh's house, but he should have known it would be uncomfortable for Sarai to be treated as an available woman when she wasn't. What kind of man does that to his wife so that he can be "treated well?" Abram willingly sold and took

33

a dowry for Sarai, as if she were available for marriage (some people might call this pimping). The Bible doesn't tell us what all Sarah had to endure while in Pharaoh's house, and the Bible also doesn't tell us how long Sarai was in Pharaoh's house before God inflected, *"serious diseases on Pharaoh and his household"* (Genesis 12:17). However, the Bible does tell us that Pharaoh confronted Abram; Abram confessed to the deceit, and Pharaoh kicked him out of the country but allowed him to keep his possessions. So Abram and Sarai continued on their journey.

Twenty-four years later, at the age of ninety-nine, Abram would have an encounter with God that resulted in his name being changed to Abraham, and Sarai's name being changed to Sarah. During the encounter God promised him that he would have descendants too numerous to count and that Sarah would produce a child in her old age:

> *Then God added, "Regarding Sarai, your wife—her name will no longer be Sarai; from now on you will call her Sarah. And I will bless her and give you a son from her! Yes, I will bless her richly, and she will become the mother of many nations. Kings will be among her descendants!"* (Genesis 17:15-16, NLT).

And wouldn't you know it. Abraham once again asked Sarah to be his sister and she agreed...again! (Genesis 20:1-18). King Abimelech took Sarah into his home, but God appeared to him in a dream and let him know that she was a married woman. Abimelech confronted Abraham and he came up with a sorry excuse for his action:

> *"Well," Abraham said, "I figured this was a godless place. I thought, 'They will want my wife and will kill me to get her.' Besides she is my sister—we both have the same father, though different mothers—and I married her.*

Chapter Three — Liar, Liar, Pants On Fire!

When God sent me to travel far from my father's home, I told her, 'Wherever we go, have the kindness to say that you are my sister'" (Genesis 20:11-13, NLT).

Abimelech sent him away with sheep, cattle and a thousand shekels of silver, and never touched Sarah. This is an important point because God had promised Abraham and Sarah a child (Genesis 12:7) and He didn't want there to be any confusion regarding parentage.

Sarai didn't realize that God's timing and our timing isn't the same. She waited and waited to get pregnant and nothing happened. Then she decided to take matters into her own hands by suggesting to Abram that he take Hagar as his second wife and sleep with her, which he did. That action alone may have caused some friction, but the real trouble started when Hagar became pregnant. Sarai believed that Hagar was throwing the pregnancy in her face and she didn't like it:

Then Sarai said to Abram "It's all your fault! Now this servant of mine is pregnant, and she despises me, though I myself gave her the privilege of sleeping with you. The Lord will make you pay for doing this to me!" Abram replied, "Since she is your servant, you may do with her as you see fit." So Sarai treated her harshly...(Genesis 16:5-6, NLT).

Hagar ran away and met an angel who told her to return to Sarai and endure whatever treatment she gave her. Hagar obediently returned, delivered a son and Abram named him Ishmael.

Fourteen years later Sarah would birth Isaac, the heir to Abraham's kingdom. Once he was weaned Sarah wanted Ishmael and his mother gone: *"Get rid of that servant and her son. He is not going to share the family inheritance with my son, Isaac. I won't have it!"* (Genesis 21:10, NLT). Abraham had grown fond of Ishmael and was distressed about Sarah's request, but God assured him that Ishmael would be taken care of:

> *This upset Abraham very much because Ishmael was his son. But God told Abraham, "Do not be upset over the boy and your servant wife. Do just as Sarah says, for Isaac is the son through whom your descendants will be counted. But I will make a nation of the descendants of Hagar's son because he also is your son"* (Genesis 21:11-13, NLT).

ISSUE #2—Why would Sarai/Sarah allow herself to be put into a position of prostitution?

Sarah appears to have willingly agreed to Abraham's charade. She never pointed out that the deception was a dangerous thing to do. She had endured the humiliation of being given to Pharaoh and then years later her husband asked her to repeat the process with Abimelech. She had to have been insulted, yet, she went along with the proposition...again. Did she enjoy her lifestyle that much that she would willingly put her self-esteem on hold? Why was she silent? We know she could be vocal, because she made very clear her feelings toward Hagar and Ishmael, so why wasn't she that vocal about being used by strange men and her husband?

Years ago model and actress Cybil Shepherd made a commercial where she said, "Don't hate me because I'm beautiful. After all, I had nothing to do with it," which is very true. If you are one of the so-called beautiful people, you certainly can't pat yourself on the back because of your looks. Short of plastic surgery, you have virtually nothing to do with the way you look. Hopefully you realize that you're

Chapter Three — Liar, Liar, Pants On Fire!

more than your looks, because looks have an uncanny way of changing.

I think that Sarah's beauty had a lot to do with her decisions. Perhaps she had been told all of her life that she was beautiful and she believed that was the only thing she had to offer. She was probably used to people only seeing a pretty face and not the woman behind the face. This might have been true especially during her barren years. She may have thought if she didn't agree with Abraham he would put her out and she would be without husband or child.

LIKE FATHER, LIKE SON, PART ONE

Isaac—the child born to Abraham and Sarah in their old age—is probably best known for being willing to be sacrificed on the altar by his father in Genesis 22:1-19. But I want to focus on his embracing his father's deceiving spirit.

When Isaac was of age, Abraham sent his servant to find him a wife. The servant prayed and asked the Lord to help him:

> *"O Lord, God of my master," he prayed. "Give me success and show kindness to my master, Abraham. Help me to accomplish the purpose of my journey. See, here I am standing beside this spring, and the young women of the village are coming out to draw water. This is my request. I will ask one of them for a drink. If she says, "Yes, certainly, and I will water your camels, too!"—let her be the one you have appointed as Isaac's wife. By this I will know that you have shown kindness to my master* (Genesis 24:12-14, NLT).

God honored his prayer and a young woman named Rebekah did exactly as the servant had asked. The servant went home with Rebekah and explained his mission to her father,

37

Bethuel, and her brother, Laban. They agreed to the marriage proposal and the servant gave the family lavish gifts sent from Abraham. The servant spent the night and when they were ready to leave the following morning, Rebekah's family wanted her to stay with them a little while longer. The servant refused their request and they started on their journey.

Isaac was walking in the fields when Rebekah and the servant arrived. He took one look at her and was smitten. They married and the Bible says that, *"He loved her very much"* (Genesis 24:67, NLT).

A famine hit the land and Isaac moved his family to Gerar where Abimelech lived. And just like his father before him, Isaac lied about Rebekah being his wife after being promised a blessing from God:

> *A severe famine now struck the land, as had happened in Abraham's time. So Isaac moved to Gerar, where Abimelech, king of the Philistines, lived. The Lord appeared to him there and said, "Do not go to Egypt. Do as I say, and stay here in this land. If you do, I will be with you and bless you. I will give all this land to you and your descendants, just as I solemnly promised Abraham, your father. I will cause your descendants to become as numerous as the stars, and I will give them all these lands. And through your descendants all the nations of the earth will be blessed. I will do this because Abraham listened to me and obeyed all of my requirements, commands, regulations and laws." So Isaac stayed in Gerar* (Genesis 26:1-6, NLT).

Isaac took a page from his father's book and told Rebekah to say that she was his sister—which was an outright lie—because he feared the men would kill him because of her

Chapter Three — Liar, Liar, Pants On Fire!

beauty (at least when Abraham used Sarah like that he was telling the truth). Unlike Abraham, though, Isaac couldn't keep his hands off of his "sister" and the king saw them caressing one another. Abimelech confronted him about it and Isaac admitted that he was afraid he would be killed because of Rebekah. Abimelech put out a decree that no one was to touch the man or his wife or they would die, and he sent Isaac and Rebekah on their way.

COMPARISONS ARE SOMETHING UNAVOIDABLE

Abraham and Isaac had several similar traits:

- Both were involved with Abimelech (Genesis 21:22-24 and Genesis 26:26-31) which resulted in a peace treaty being signed.

- Both were in a dispute over water rights although they handled their disputes differently. Abraham spoke directly with Abimelech over what was happening, which resulted in him being given ownership of the wells (Genesis 21:25-31). Isaac chose to move from location to location to location instead of fighting for what belonged to his father (Genesis 26:18-22).

- And they both lied about their wives being their sisters (Genesis 20:1-18 and Genesis 26:7-11). Basically what they told their wives were: "This is your fault! If you weren't so beautiful I wouldn't have to stoop to lying about who you are. Don't blame me because this is the only way I can protect us!" To me the problem with this thinking is pretty obvious: Sarah and Rebekah were beautiful when they met Abraham and Isaac; their looks only became an issue when they needed to save their own hides.

I GUESS THIS MEANS THE HONEYMOON IS OVER, HUH?

We don't know how long Isaac and Rebekah had been married before it became apparent she was barren. That would have been disappointing, because children were a status symbol in Old Testament times, especially if a male child was born. Isaac prayed for his wife and the Lord honored his request with not one, but two children:

> But the two children struggled with each other in her womb. So she went to ask the Lord about it. "Why is this happening to me?" she asked. And the Lord told her, "The sons in your womb will become two rival nations. One nation will be stronger than the other; the descendants of your older son will serve the descendants of your younger son." And when the time came, the twins were born. The first was very red at birth. He was covered with so much hair that one would think he was wearing a piece of clothing. So they called him Esau. Then the other twin was born with his hand grasping Esau's heel. So they called him Jacob (Genesis 25:22-26, NLT).

The twins weren't identical in either looks or personality. The Bible takes them from newborns to adult men so we are not provided insight into their childhood. What we do discover is that Esau liked to hunt and Jacob liked to stay close to home. We are also told that Isaac loved Esau and that Rebekah loved Jacob.

One day Jacob was cooking and Esau came in from the field famished. He asked for something to eat and Jacob agreed, but only after successfully negotiating Esau's birthright away from him. Esau either wasn't aware of the impor-

Chapter Three — Liar, Liar, Pants On Fire!

tance of being the first-born or he didn't care; either way he willingly sold his birthright to Jacob for a bowl of stew. Isaac was very wealthy and Jacob would have been provided with a substantial inheritance upon his father's death; evidently this wasn't enough for a greedy person like Jacob.

When Isaac was old and blind, he wanted to bestow a blessing on Esau before he died. He called him in and requested that he catch and prepare wild game for him. Esau agreed and went to do his father's bidding. In the meantime Rebekah had overheard Isaac's request and convinced Jacob to impersonate Esau, even though Jacob was at first reluctant:

> *"But Mother!" Jacob replied. "He won't be fooled that easily. Think how hairy Esau is and how smooth my skin is! What if my father touches me? He'll see that I'm trying to trick him, and then he'll curse me instead of blessing me." "Let the curse fall on me, dear son," said Rebekah. "Just do what I tell you. Go out and get the goats." So Jacob followed his mother's instructions...* (Genesis 27:11-14(a), NLT).

We will never know all the reasons Rebekah chose to deceive her husband, but Isaac was fooled into bestowing the blessing intended for Esau onto Jacob. When Esau found out about it, he threatened to kill his brother. Rebekah told Jacob to go to her brother Laban's house to hide. Rebekah told Isaac that the reason for sending Jacob away was to find a suitable wife because she didn't want him making the same mistake Esau had (Esau had married two Hittite women who were a source of grief for Rebekah and Isaac (Genesis 26:34-35)). Isaac agreed to Rebekah's request not knowing that by doing so he was unwittingly setting the stage for the next dramatic chapter in this family's life.

Chapter Four —
The Professor Is In

As we discovered in the previous chapter, deception was passed down from Abraham to Isaac and, unfortunately, it didn't stop there. Jacob inherited and embraced the family's deceptive spirit and took it to a new level; a master's class was just about to begin.

Jacob had to leave his home because he and his mother had tricked his father, Isaac, into giving him something that didn't belong to him. His mother told Jacob to go to her brother's house in Haran to get away from his brother, Esau's, wrath because of the trickery. When Jacob arrived in Haran, he went to the water hole and asked the men who were there if they knew his uncle, Laban. They told him they did and that his daughter was coming toward them with her sheep. The stone to the well was usually not rolled away until all of the sheep had arrived, but because Rachel was a relative Jacob rolled the stone away for her to water the sheep. He then told Rachel who he was; she ran home to tell her father and Laban came out to greet him. Jacob went home with Laban and his family.

After a month of working for Laban, he asked Jacob how much money he wanted as payment. Because Jacob had felt the thunderbolt of love upon looking at Rachel, he asked for her hand in marriage and offered to work seven years for her. Laban agreed and Jacob got busy. Upon fulfillment of his contract the marriage was performed.

Jacob had been right to expect retribution from God for the part he played in deceiving his father out of the blessing. But the curse Jacob feared wasn't death; it was something more perfidious because he didn't realize that payback was coming. See, the problem with payback is that you never know when, how or where it is going to occur, but before you take your final breath you are going to reap what you sow.

Jacob entered the marriage tent excited and happy. He had waited seven years for the love of his life and his patience was about to pay off. Little did he know that Laban was every bit as tricky as he was and he had no problem manipulating things in his favor.

On his wedding night Jacob laid with who he thought was Rachel only to discover the next morning that it was Leah, which begs to ask several questions: Since Jacob had been around both Leah and Rachel for seven years, why couldn't he tell the difference between the two women in the dark? And why was it dark? Don't most bridegrooms want to look at their brides? The Bible says that Rachel was both beautiful and shapely, which would indicate that Leah wasn't. Didn't he touch her? Didn't he recognize that their voices weren't the same? Questions, questions and more questions:

> *"What sort of trick is this?" Jacob raged at La-ban. "I worked seven years for Rachel. What do you mean by this trickery?" "It's not our custom to marry off a younger daughter ahead of the firstborn," Laban replied. "Wait until the bridal week is over, and you can have Rachel, too—that is if you promise to work another seven years for me." So Jacob agreed to work seven more years. A week after Jacob had married Leah, Laban gave him Rachel, too. And Laban gave Rachel a servant, Bilhah, to be her maid. So Jacob slept with Rachel, too, and he loved her more than Leah. He then stayed and worked the additional seven years* (Genesis 29:25(b)-30, NLT).

Chapter Four — The Professor Is In

There is no recorded dialogue between Leah and Rachel, but there had to be hard feelings between them. Leah was put in the middle by her father and tradition. She must have felt very small to be used to trick a man into marrying her knowing that he loved her sister. Leah didn't have anyone willing to work seven years for her, but her sister did. Did Rachel gloat about that or was she used to being shown favoritism because of her beauty? Had Leah grown up feeling "less than" because of comparisons to Rachel?

The Lord blessed Leah because she wasn't loved by her husband and she had four sons in quick succession: Reuben, Simeon, Levi and Judah (Genesis 29:31-35). Leah reminds me of something a friend of mine once said, "Honey, all my husband has to do is look at me and I get pregnant!" Obviously there is more involved in getting pregnant, but my friend's point is that she is very fertile; it didn't take a whole lot of effort to conceive. Leah appears to have been the same way.

When Rachel saw that she wasn't having any children, she became jealous of her sister:

> *"Give me children, or I'll die!" she exclaimed to Jacob. Jacob flew into a rage. "Am I God?" he asked. "He is the only one able to give you children!"* (Genesis 30:1-2, NLT).

Rachel didn't like his answer and gave him her servant, Bilhah, to sleep with and their union would produce two sons: Dan and Naphtali. In the meantime, it appeared that Leah's baby-making days were over so she had Jacob sleep with her servant, Zilpah, who presented Jacob with two more sons, Gad and Asher. Whew! Jacob was certainly a busy man!

During the wheat harvest, Leah's oldest son, Reuben, found some mandrakes growing in the field and took them to his mother. Mandrakes were believed to be a cure for sterility. When Rachel heard about them she asked Leah for

45

some, but Leah refused to share. Rachel offered Jacob for one night in exchange for the mandrakes and Leah agreed. The Bible suggests that Leah had also eaten some of the mandrakes because she would have two more sons: Issachar and Zebulun, and a daughter named Dinah (Genesis 30:14-24).

The Bible also suggests that Rachel's scheming was unnecessary. After the birth of Leah's three children, the Bible says:

> *Then God remembered Rachel's plight and answered her prayers by giving her a child. She became pregnant and gave birth to a son. "God has removed my shame," she said. And she named him Joseph, for she said, "May the Lord give me yet another son"* (Genesis 30:22-24, NIV).

WILL THE MASTER DECEIVER PLEASE STAND UP

Years ago there was a game show called *To Tell the Truth.* The object of the game was to guess which of the three participants were telling the truth about their identity. The concept for the show must have come from this story in Genesis.

Shortly after the birth of his son with the love of his life, Jacob wanted to go home. He went to Laban requesting permission to leave, but Laban wanted him to stay because, *"The Lord has blessed me because you are here"* (Genesis 30:27, NLT). Laban told him to name whatever price he wanted in order to keep him. Jacob pointed out that he had faithfully served Laban and the Lord blessed Laban because of everything Jacob was doing. But Jacob wanted to provide for his family on his own. Laban didn't want to hear that and asked him again what it would take for him to stay:

Chapter Four — The Professor Is In

"Don't give me anything at all. Just do one thing, and I'll go back to work for you. Let me go out among your flocks today and remove all the sheep and goats that are speckled or spotted, along with all the dark-colored sheep. Give them to me as my wages. This will make it easy for you to see whether or not I have been honest. If you find in my flock any white sheep or goats that are not speckled, you will know that I have stolen them from you." "All right," Laban replied. "It will be as you have said" (Genesis 30:31(b)-34, NLT).

It is always interesting to listen to con artists talk among themselves because each one thinks they are the slickest. Laban thought he was clever, but he didn't realize that Jacob was the author of *The Trickster's Handbook*. On the surface it seemed that Jacob accepted Laban's agreement regarding the sheep and goats, but in the back of his mind Jacob had to be remembering that this was the same man who had tricked him with Leah. While Laban was plotting how to keep Jacob from leaving, Jacob was scheming how to make the spotted sheep and goats stronger which would increase his flock and his wealth (Genesis 30:35-43). Most schemes eventually get discovered and this one was no different. Laban's sons began to grumble about Jacob, and Jacob noticed that Laban's attitude toward him had changed. The Lord told him to return to his father's land, and he began making plans to leave. He told Leah and Rachel what was going on:

Rachel and Leah said, "That's fine with us! There's nothing for us here—none of our father's wealth will come to us anyway. He has reduced our rights to those of foreign women. He sold us, and what he received for us has

47

disappeared. The riches God has given you from our father are legally ours and our children's to begin with. So go ahead and do whatever God has told you" (Genesis 31:14-16, NLT).

Jacob packed up his wives, children, possessions and left. Rachel decided she would relieve her father of some of his household possessions and put them with her stuff. They had been gone three days before Laban discovered their absence. He took off after them and found them a week later:

"What do you mean by sneaking off like this?" Laban demanded. "Are my daughters prisoners, the plunder of war, that you have stolen them away like this? Why did you slip away secretly? I would have given you a farewell party, with joyful singing accompanied by tambourines and harps. Why didn't you let me kiss my daughters and grandchildren and tell them good-bye? You have acted very foolishly! I could destroy you, but the God of your father appeared to me last night and told me, 'Be careful about what you say to Jacob!' I know you feel you must go, and you long intensely for your childhood home, but why have you stolen my household gods?" (Genesis 31:26-30, NLT).

Since Jacob was in the dark about Rachel's actions, he could honestly admit that he didn't know what Laban was talking about and offered for whoever had stolen his property to be killed. Rachel had hidden the items in her saddlebags and was sitting on them. When everything and everyone else was searched, she said she was having her menstrual cycle and no one touched her. (The law stated

Chapter Four — The Professor Is In

that anyone who touched a woman or anything she sat on during her cycle would be unclean, Leviticus 15:19-20). Jacob and Laban resolved their differences by making a peace treaty and Laban kissed his daughters and grandchildren goodbye. He sent them away with his blessings and returned home.

Jacob knew that in order to go home he would have to pass through territory belonging to his brother, Esau, the man he and his mother had tricked out of his birthright and blessing. He was understandably nervous and came up with a plan that he thought would appease Esau. He chose two hundred ewes, twenty rams, thirty female camels with their young, forty cows, ten bulls, twenty female donkeys and ten male donkeys and sent them ahead with his servants (Genesis 32:15-16). Then he gave specific instructions to his servants:

> *"When you meet Esau, he will ask, 'Where are you going? Whose servants are you? Whose animals are these?' You should reply, 'These belong to your servant Jacob. They are a present for his master Esau! He is coming right behind us.' Jacob gave the same instructions to each of the herdsmen...* (Genesis 32:17-19(a), NLT).

The next morning as Jacob saw Esau coming toward him with four hundred men he arranged his family as follows: He would be in the lead with his two concubines and their children directly behind him. Leah and her children were to be next, and Rachel and Joseph were last. The placement is important because once again it shows the preference of Rachel over Leah. If a battle actually ensued, Rachel and Joseph would most likely be the last hurt. Fortunately, all of Jacob's plotting was unnecessary. He and Esau made peace. Esau returned back to Seir and Jacob continued on until he arrived at Shechem in Canaan.

LIKE FATHER, LIKE SON, PART TWO

There are some family traits you want to pass onto your children and some you don't. Jacob was a deceiver. He had the ability to convince you that he was sincere in what he was saying, and then when you believed him, the truth would come out. This smooth talking ability was obviously inherited by his sons, Simeon and Levi. A prince saw Jacob's daughter, liked what he saw, grabbed her and raped her:

> But Shechem's love for Dinah was strong, and he tried to win her affection. He even spoke to his father about it. "Get this girl for me," he demanded. "I want to marry her" (Genesis 34:3-4, NLT).

Hamor, Shechem's father, went to Jacob to discuss the matter just as Dinah's brothers were coming in from the field. When they heard about what happened to their sister, they were understandably angry. Hamor pleaded his son's case and pointed out that he wanted to marry Dinah. Shechem had gone with his father to see Jacob and he also pleaded his case. The brothers talked among themselves and then told Hamor and Shechem that in order for the union to take place all of the men would have to be circumcised. They pointed out that this was the only way they would allow Dinah to intermarry; otherwise, they were going to be on their way and the prince would never see Dinah again. Hamor and his father readily agreed and the procedure took place:

> But three days later, when their wounds were still sore, two of Dinah's brothers, Simeon and Levi, took their swords, entered the town without opposition, and slaughtered

Chapter Four — The Professor Is In

*every man there, including Hamor and She-
chem. They rescued Dinah from Shechem's
house and returned to their camp. Then all of
Jacob's sons plundered the town because
their sister had been defiled there. They
seized all the flocks and herds and donkeys—everything they could lay their hands
on, both inside the town and outside in the
fields. They also took all the women and
children and wealth of every kind. Afterward
Jacob said to Levi and Simeon, "You have
made me stink among all the people of this
land—among all the Canaanites and Periz-
zites. We are so few that they will come and
crush us. We will all be killed!" "Should he
treat our sister like a prostitute?" they re-
torted angrily* (Genesis 34:25-31, NLT).

God told Jacob to pack up and leave and he and his household headed for Bethel. Once they arrived in the land of
Canaan, God changed Jacob's name to Israel (Genesis
35:10). Rachel became pregnant with their second child and
would die shortly after his birth. She named him Ben-Oni,
"Son of My Trouble," but Israel changed his name to Benjamin, "Son of My Right Hand." Rachel would be buried on
the way to Bethlehem (Genesis 35:18-19).

Jacob went home to Hebron and was there when his
father, Isaac, died at the age of one hundred and eighty
years old. Jacob had passed on his deceiving spirit to his
sons who entered into an agreement to commit murder to
avenge their sister. As we will see in the next chapter, that
murderous spirit never left them. Jacob and his family
remained in the land of Canaan, where the curtain is about
to go up on the next chapter of this familial saga.

51

Chapter Five —
Wait!
You Haven't Heard The Whole Story Yet

Do you remember I said in chapter three that I always ask the same question when I read the story of Joseph and his brothers: How could they betray their own flesh and blood, and I said I didn't believe there is any one answer to this question? There isn't, but there are some mitigating factors that I think will help us better understand where the brothers were emotionally when they agreed to such drastic action. However, that doesn't make their decision right; they were wrong and there is no justifying what they did.

I have often asked parents of multiple children whether or not they have a favorite child, and they usually respond by saying that they try to love their children equally and not show favoritism. However, when I ask people with siblings whether or not they believed their parents have a favorite child, they almost unanimously reply, "Yes!"

I think that wise parents of multiple children learn to value each child for their own uniqueness and not try to make them into something they are not. While growing up I always heard my father say, "Why can't you be more like your sister?" which was very irritating. Of course, I grew up in an era where children didn't talk back to their parents so I had to keep my comments to myself. What I wanted to say was that I can't be like my sister, because she is who she is and I am who I am!

I have three sisters and two brothers. My mother spread her love equally among us, but I can unequivocally tell you that my father wasn't as democratic. My second oldest sister was my father's favorite because she looked the most like my mother and her side of the family, whereas the rest of my siblings and I look like my father and his side of the family. Even though I recognized that my sister was favored, it never occurred to me to plot with my other siblings to get rid of her! (Actually, we learned to take advantage of it in that if we wanted to do something, we just got her to ask our father and the request was usually granted). To this day there is no sibling rivalry; it wasn't her fault my father favored her, so we learned to live with it.

LITTLE PITCHERS HAVE BIG EARS

This familiar saying means that children see and hear more than we give them credit for.

When I was the leader of the single parents' ministry at my church, one of the things I always encouraged the members to be careful about was discussing their child's other parent around them, especially if the relationship was less than ideal. Kids are like sponges in that they absorb everything. One thing I will always be grateful for is that God, even before I accepted Him into my life, told me not to ever say anything negative about my son's father. When my son was little and began to question why other kids had a father and he didn't, I always answered his questions honestly: He did have a father; he just didn't live with us. Any feelings my son have toward his father are his own, not what I have told him he should feel.

Leah, Bilhah and Zilpah inadvertently fueled the acrimony between Joseph and his brothers. The brothers took their mothers' side because they could see they were miserable. They may have heard them crying softly at night after Jacob left their bed. They may have overheard them talking among themselves about how Jacob treated Rachel better than them. Or they may have noticed the look of despair in their mothers' eyes when they thought no one was watching. Who knows what all went into the rivalry; their mothers' treatment was definitely a sore point for the brothers.

Chapter Five — Wait! You Haven't Heard The Whole Story Yet

IF YOU THINK SOMEBODY'S WATCHING YOU, YOU'RE RIGHT

In order to fully understand how siblings could agree to conspire against one of their own, as in the case of Joseph and his brothers, you have to go to the beginning of the story. And the story begins with the love triangle of Leah, Rachel and Jacob. We have already looked at their history in the previous chapter. In this chapter I want to look at the results of their actions upon their children. Just like peeling an onion reveals layer after layer, there is more to the story of the brothers' betrayal than what we normally study. There is no denying that Jacob's favoritism toward Joseph wasn't handled correctly. But that is because he was in love.

Jacob was ecstatic because Rachel, the love of his life, didn't just give him a child; she gave him a male child. It is amazing to look into the face of a child you have created with another person and notice your reflection in their face and/or mannerisms—your nose, your spouse's eyes, your grandfather's ears and your mother's temperament. All of that was true for Jacob as well, and while he may have paid attention to those details with Leah, Bilhah and Zilpah's children, he took special note of those traits in his true love's child. Jacob lavished attention on Joseph, gave him special gifts and probably started the majority of his conversations with, "Joseph said..." or "Joseph did..."

I think his brothers could have overlooked that if it hadn't been for the fact that Jacob was emotionally abusing their mothers by withholding his love. Emotional abuse is abuse, too. So while Jacob didn't beat his wives, and he provided them with food, clothing and shelter, he deprived them of his love and affection.

You would think that if Jacob was going to lavish attention on any of his children it would have been his first-born son (and not the first-born son with Rachel), but Reuben was produced with Leah, and despite sleeping with her I am not sure that Jacob ever fully forgave her for agreeing to go along with Laban's plan to trick him. That is an irrational feeling on his part since Leah didn't have a lot of say-so in the matter. She was under her father's authority, which doesn't necessarily mean that she wanted to do as she was ordered. But even knowing the truth sometimes doesn't prevent you from feeling what you feel, whether it is irrational or not. Jacob took one look at Rachel and fell in love, and his feelings never changed.

Joseph's brothers probably wouldn't have paid that much attention to any of that except that they had observed their mothers' suffering from the lack of Jacob's love. I am sure he was fond of them, but most women don't want "fondness" from their husband. Leah, Bilhah and Zilpah learned the hard way that sex and love are not the same. Perhaps they had resigned themselves to the fact that Jacob didn't care that much about them until they saw him with Rachel and Joseph. Up to that point they may have convinced themselves he was just undemonstrative. Perhaps they thought he was incapable of showing his feelings outside the bed chamber. Perhaps he never displayed passion with the others. Whatever they thought was his malfunction was quickly dispelled when they saw Jacob interact with Rachel. Then it became obvious that not only could Jacob be demonstrative, but also that he really did love Rachel. He treated her differently; his face lit up when she walked into a room, his voice took on a husky timber when he spoke to her, his touch was more intimate than with the other women. It didn't take an Einstein to figure out that there was something different about their relationship, even before Rachel gave him a male child. Rachel had that glow that comes from knowing that you are loved. That is a hard pill to swallow, especially for Leah who was an innocent pawn in this fiasco.

It takes time to get to such a level of dislike that you plot a person's demise. You don't wake up one day and decide you hate your brother; that emotion builds and

Chapter Five — Wait! You Haven't Heard The Whole Story Yet

festers, festers and builds, until it boils over to the point you can't stand the sight of them or to hear their voice.

Most of Joseph's brothers were grown when he was born, and they had a long time to observe Jacob's behavior with their mothers. They hadn't forgotten that Rachel and Joseph were placed at the end of the caravan to meet Esau, as if their lives were more important than anyone else's. They hadn't forgotten that Jacob treated Joseph as if he were the first-born and not Reuben, who was the rightful heir apparent. They hadn't forgotten that Jacob gave Joseph a special coat and he wore it all the time, strutting around as if he were better than the others. See, Joseph had the same glow Rachel had because he knew he was loved. Sometimes when you are treated in a special way you become insensitive to the fact that not everyone is experiencing the same level of treatment. Joseph knew only love from his father and he assumed that his brothers were receiving the same kind of attention.

Sometimes parents mean well, but those subtle differences in behavior aren't always forgotten. I have noticed sometimes how people treat biological and non-biological children differently in a blended or extended family. There is a shift in behavior and attitude; it is not always blatant and could easily be overlooked. Whenever I have observed this behavior I have often wanted to ask the child how they feel about the way they are being treated.

Joseph was already favored and probably had even more affection bestowed upon him after Rachel died shortly after giving birth to Benjamin. Jacob held special affection for Benjamin because he, too, was a product of his union with Rachel, but whenever Jacob looked at Benjamin he couldn't help but remember that his beloved was dead, although it wasn't Benjamin's fault. Joseph probably still received the lion's share of Jacob's affection because there was no death stigma attached to him:

Jacob loved Joseph more than any of his other children because Joseph had been born to him in his old age. So one day Jacob had a special gift made for Joseph—a beautiful robe. But his brothers hated Joseph because their father loved him more than the rest of them. They couldn't say a kind word to him (Genesis 37:3-4, NLT).

Joseph's brothers disliked him because of Jacob's favoritism, but also because Joseph was a tattle-tale. The Bible says that he brought his father reports of what his brothers were doing (Genesis 37:2(a) and when Jacob sent Joseph out to look for his brothers the day they dropped him in the well, Jacob had specifically told him to bring back a report about them (Genesis 37:14). Nobody likes someone spying on them, and Joseph probably wasn't very good at hiding what he was doing. The final straw for the brothers was when Joseph began sharing dreams about his superiority. When you already don't like someone, you certainly don't want to hear about how you are going to bow down to them! The brothers saw Joseph coming toward them and snapped. That is the only reasonable explanation for purposely plotting to kill him.

LIKE FATHER, LIKE SON, PART THREE

Abraham passed on a deceiving spirit to Isaac, who then passed it to Jacob, who then passed it to his children. Are you noticing a pattern here? When the brothers plotted to kill Joseph, Reuben talked them out of it and instead proposed they put him down a well. His intention was to go back later, retrieve Joseph from the well and take him home. Unfortunately, when Reuben got back to the well the brothers had decided to sell him for twenty shekels (eight ounces) of silver!

Chapter Five — Wait! You Haven't Heard The Whole Story Yet

You have probably heard the expression that there is no honor among thieves? Well, there is also no honor among deceivers. How do I know? When Reuben asked his brothers what had happened to Joseph, they never answered his question, but instead suggested that they take Joseph's multi-colored coat, slather it with animal blood and present it to Jacob for identification. When Jacob concluded that an animal had indeed killed Joseph, the brothers never corrected their father's thinking (Genesis 37:19-33).

WE NOW COME TO THE CLOSE OF OUR DRAMA

Unbeknownst to Jacob and his sons, Joseph was experiencing a series of mishaps—including prison—which were moving him closer to his destiny. While still incarcerated Joseph had interpreted Pharaoh's dream that there would be seven years of feast and seven years of famine in Egypt. As a reward Joseph was released from prison and promoted to governor. Although he didn't realize it at the time, he was in the right place at the right time for God to initiate a family reunion.

During the seven years of feast, Joseph wisely instructed the people to put up grain for when the famine came. When the famine did occur, Egypt was the only place to go for food. Jacob, still in Canaan, sent his sons to Egypt to purchase food, *"But Jacob wouldn't let Joseph's younger brother, Benjamin, go with them, for fear some harm might come to him"* (Genesis 42:4, NLT). So the brothers, minus Benjamin, went to Egypt.

You would think that if you had thrown somebody in a well and then sold them as a slave that you would at least remember what they looked like, right? Not so. Joseph recognized his brothers, but they didn't have a clue as to who he was. (Granted, the last time they saw Joseph he was a teenager, but still). Anyway, the brothers made their request for food, but Joseph would only sell it to them if he

59

were allowed to keep Simeon as collateral and they returned with their youngest brother, Benjamin. The brothers went back home trying to figure out the best way to break this news to Jacob who they knew would be upset. Jacob listened to them in astonishment:

> "...My son will not go down with you. His brother Joseph is dead, and he is all I have left. If anything should happen to him on your journey, you would send this grieving white-haired man to his grave" (Genesis 42:38, NLT).

Jacob never did learn how to effectively parent a blended family. While Joseph was still at home, he showered affection on him to the point of making his brothers jealous. When he believed that Joseph had died, he then turned his affection toward Benjamin; the only surviving (or so he thought) child of the union between he and Rachel. Fortunately, the brothers had taken anger management classes and didn't respond to this blatant favoritism of Benjamin the way they had with Joseph. Perhaps by this time they had gotten used to it and just accepted that their father wasn't going to change. Either way it goes, they didn't abuse their brother.

The Bible doesn't specify how much time elapsed before all of the grain they purchased in Egypt the first time was used up. When it was gone, Jacob wanted his sons to go back to get more food, but Judah reminded him of Joseph's stipulation. Jacob finally relented and the brothers returned to Egypt with Benjamin. Joseph was overwhelmed when he saw his younger brother; he threw a feast for all of them, seated his brothers according to their ages and gave Benjamin five times as much as the others (Genesis 43).

When the feast was over, Joseph revealed himself to his brothers. They were, of course, shocked and fearful. Once they got over the initial fear, Joseph told them to go

Chapter Five — Wait! You Haven't Heard The Whole Story Yet

back and bring Jacob and all of his possessions to Egypt to live; Joseph would take care of them. Jacob lived in Egypt seventeen years and died at the age of one hundred and forty-seven. Before he died, he blessed all of his sons and gave instructions for his burial:

> *Then Jacob told them, "Soon I will die. Bury me with my father and grandfather in the cave in Ephron's field...there Abraham and his wife Sarah are buried. There Isaac and his wife, Rebekah, are buried. And there I buried Leah. It is the cave that my grandfather Abraham bought from the Hitties." Then when Jacob had finished this charge to his sons, he lay back in the bed, breathed his last, and died (Genesis 49:29, 31-33, NIV).*

Did you note that Leah was buried in a place of honor in the ancestral plot? It is possible that after Rachel died, Jacob turned to Leah for comfort. Whatever his reasoning for selecting this spot for her, I am sure that if you asked Leah she would tell you that she would much rather have had his love while she was alive to appreciate it! Who knows how the story might have played out if he had?

Once Jacob was buried, the brothers were apprehensive about how Joseph would treat them. And, once again, they agreed to lie:

> *Your father left these instructions before he died: 'This is what you are to say to Joseph: I ask you to forgive your brothers the sins and the wrongs they committed in treating you so badly.' Now please forgive the sins of the servants of the God of your father." When their message came to him, Joseph wept (Genesis 50:16-1, NIV).*

Joseph assured his brothers that he didn't hold any animosity against them. They were wrong; Joseph knew they were wrong, and Joseph knew that they knew they were wrong. That was enough for him. But just to make sure they understood where he was coming from, he gave them something to think about:

> *"Don't be afraid. Am I in the place of God? You intended to harm me, **but God** intended it for good to accomplish what is now being done, the saving of many lives"* (Genesis 50:19-20, NIV, emphasis mine).

Have you ever had a "But God" moment in your life? A moment so insightful where everything becomes crystal clear? Joseph's moment allowed him to treat his brothers graciously, despite their hatred. He could have told them, "Yeah, I know you tried to kill me. You heard me hollering from the well and calmly sat down to eat. You didn't even have the decency to throw a piece of meat down to me. You hated me so much that you sold your own brother because you couldn't handle my favor! Yeah, you meant to harm me, but God wouldn't let you. And you better never stop thanking God that he won't let me treat you the way you treated me. So, don't worry about it. It's over. It's done. It's forgotten. Dad's dead and buried, but I'll still take care of you, because I'm a bigger and better man that any of you will ever be!"

Joseph lived to be one hundred and ten years old. The Bible records the one time Joseph asked his brothers for a favor:

> *"...I am ready to die. God will most certainly pay you a visit and take you out of this land and back to the land he so solemnly promised to Abraham, Isaac and Jacob." Then Joseph made the sons of Israel promise under oath,*

Chapter Five — Wait! You Haven't Heard The Whole Story Yet

> *"When God makes his visitation, make sure you take my bones with you as you leave here"* (Genesis 50:24-26, The Message).

And the brothers finally did something right! When their descendants left Egypt several hundred years later, Joseph's bones went with them (Exodus 13:19).

The next time your family gets on your nerves, I want you to remember that it could always be worse. Abraham, Isaac and Jacob's legacies include a lot of life lessons of what to do as well as what not to do. It would behoove us to pay attention and learn from them.

Chapter Six —
Sisters On A Mission

As a child I would delay asking my father for anything until the very last minute. The reason I did that was because I knew that before he would respond, I was going to have to answer what, in my humble opinion, were a lot of unnecessary questions. The questioning wouldn't have been so bad if I had known he would answer in the positive, but that usually was not the case and, consequently, I stopped asking for stuff. While that wasn't a very mature way to handle things, it was one sure way of making sure I wasn't disappointed with a negative answer.

Have you ever avoided asking for something you really wanted because you thought the answer would be no? Did you convince yourself that it would be a waste of time to ask? Did you even think that maybe what you were asking for was so far out of reach that you had no business asking for it in the first place? Was what you wanted so big that you didn't share the desire with anyone for fear of being ridiculed?

Well, if you answered yes to any of these questions, there is a story in the Bible where your name would fit perfectly. Five biological sisters—Mahlah, Noah, Hoglah, Milcah and Tirzah—joined in agreement and subsequently changed history, and they did it because God recognized and admired their audaciousness in asking for what they wanted. While I am sure that getting to the final agreement stage involved a lot of discussion—after all, we are talking about five women with five distinct personalities—one fact remains true: Sometimes God is just waiting for us to ask the right question, in the right way, so that He is then freed up to work on our behalf.

Obieray Rogers

HISTORY IN THE MAKING

Mahlah, Noah, Hoglah, Milcah and Tirzah were the daughters of Zelophehad, belonging to the clan of Manasseh, the son of Joseph. According to biblical law, when Zelophehad died his property would have passed to his sons; however, he didn't have any. What he had were five forward-thinking women who asked for what they believed to rightly belong to them. They could have accepted the status quo, but instead put their heads together and came up with a plan to ask for their father's property. I am sure they were nervous and not as confident as they could have been going before Moses, Eleazar, the leaders and the whole assembly (Numbers 27:2), but long before the phrase "just the facts" became part of our vocabulary, these women knew that if they succinctly presented their case without a lot of histrionics, their request would at least be considered. Their plan was bold and courageous, and set in motion a precedent that would be carried out for future generations:

> Our father died in the desert. He was not among Korah's followers, who banded together against the Lord, but he died for his own sin and left no sons. Why should our father's name disappear from his clan because he had no son? Give us property among our father's relatives (Numbers 27:3-4, NIV).

The five sisters pointed out that their father wasn't part of Korah's followers because they didn't want Moses or the others to have any preconceived notions about their father or the meaning behind their request.

THE KORAH INSURGENCE

Some of the people named in the Bible received their notoriety for the wrong reasons. Korah is one such person. His

66

Chapter Six — Sisters On A Mission

story begins in Numbers chapter three when God assigned responsibility regarding the care and service of the tabernacle. God's instructions to Moses were to:

- Appoint Aaron and his sons to serve as priests; anyone else who approached the sanctuary was to be put to death (Numbers 3:10).

- Gershon (son of Levi) and the Gershonite clan were to be responsible for the care of the tabernacle and tent, its coverings, the curtain at the entrance to the Tent of Meeting, the curtains of the courtyard, the curtain at the entrance to the courtyard surrounding the tabernacle and altar, and the ropes and everything related to their use (Numbers 3:17, 25-26).

- Kohath (son of Levi and Korah's grandfather) and the Kohathite clan were to be responsible for the care of the ark, the table, the lampstand, the altars, the articles of the sanctuary used in ministering, the curtain, and everything related to their use (Numbers 3:17, 30-31).

- Merari (son of Levi) and the Merarite clan were to be responsible for taking care of the frames of the tabernacle, its crossbars, posts, bases, all its equipment and everything related to their use, as well as the posts of the surrounding courtyard with their bases, tent pegs and ropes (Numbers 3:17, 36-37).

- The chief leader of the Levites was Eleazar, son of Aaron, the priest. He was appointed over those who were responsible for the care of the sanctuary (Numbers 3:32).

Korah, his friends: Dathan, Abiram and On, and two hundred and fifty community leaders challenged Moses and

Aaron's authority to the priesthood. Korah questioned why Moses and Aaron, *"...set themselves above the Lord's assembly"* (Numbers 16:3(b)). Moses told Korah:

> *Now listen, you Levites! Isn't it enough for you that the God of Israel has separated you from the rest of the Israelite community and brought you near himself to do the work at the Lord's tabernacle and to stand before the community and minister to them? He has brought you and all your fellow Levites near himself, but now you are trying to get the priesthood too. It is against the Lord that you and all your followers have banded together. Who is Aaron that you should grumble against him?* (Numbers 16:8-11, NIV).

Moses then summoned Dathan and Abiram:

> *...But they said, 'We will not come! Isn't it enough that you have brought us up out of a land flowing with milk and honey to kill us in the desert? And now you also want to lord it over us? Moreover, you haven't brought us into a land flowing with milk and honey or given us an inheritance of fields and vineyards. Will you gouge out the eyes of these men? No, we will not come!"* (Numbers 16:12-14, NIV).

Moses wasn't pleased with their response and urged the Lord to refuse their offering. He instructed Korah and his people to meet the following day; each man was to put incense in his censer and present it before the Lord. Korah and Aaron were to present their censers also. When they all gathered the following morning, the Lord appeared to the assembly and told Moses and Aaron to separate themselves from the people so, *"I can put an end to them at once"* (Num-

Chapter Six — Sisters On A Mission

bers 16:21, NIV). Moses and Aaron interceded and the Lord relented from killing all of the people, but told Moses and Aaron to move the people away from Korah, Dathan and Abiram. Moses told the people how they would know that he had been sent by God:

> *"If these men die a natural death and experience only what usually happens to men, then the Lord has not sent me. But if the Lord brings about something totally new, and the earth opens its mouth and swallows them, with everything that belongs to them, and they go down alive in the grave, then you will know that these men have treated the Lord with contempt." As soon as he finished saying all this, the ground under them split apart and the earth opened its mouth and swallowed them, with their households and all Korah's men and all their possessions. They went down alive into the grave, with everything they owned, the earth closed over them, and they perished and were gone from the community. At their cries, all the Israelites around them fled, shouting, "The earth is going to swallow us too!" And fire came out from the Lord and consumed the 250 men who were offering the incense* (Numbers 16:29-35, NIV).

I don't know how you feel about it, but I would think that if you had witnessed something this powerful no one would ever have another problem out of you. But the children of Israel were nothing if not rebellious at heart and they still hadn't learned their lesson. The day after the execution they were back to grumbling against Moses and Aaron, *"You have killed the Lord's people, they said"* (Numbers 16:41, NIV). When they turned toward the Tent of Meeting, they discovered that the cloud covered it and the glory of the Lord appeared. The Lord told Moses that he was going to eliminate them all at once, but Moses and Aaron once again interceded on their behalf. The Lord brought a plague against the people, and by the time it was finished, *"...14,700 people died from the plague, in addition to those who had died because of Korah"* (Numbers 16:49, NIV).

THE ANSWER TO THE QUESTION

Moses took Mahlah, Noah, Hoglah, Milcah and Tirzah's petition before the Lord and the Lord agreed with their request. He gave Moses new instructions for all of the people:

> *"Say to the Israelites, 'If a man dies and leaves no son, turn his inheritance over to his daughter. If he has no daughter, give his inheritance to his brothers. If he has no brothers, give his inheritance to his father's brothers. If his father had no brothers, give his inheritance to the nearest relative in his clan, that he may possess it. This is to be a legal requirement for the Israelites, as the Lord commanded Moses'"* (Numbers 27:8-11, NIV).

Stepping out in faith and asking for what they wanted resulted in the sisters obtaining not just a blessing for themselves, but for every woman of every tribe. Nothing would have happened if they had just sat around bemoaning their fate. They would not have learned that God is a God of compassion or that He wants to provide for us.

Chapter Six — Sisters On A Mission

SOMEBODY HAS TO BE FIRST

Years ago I was a civilian employee for the Columbus Police Department (CPD) when there were no females above the rank of police officer. It hadn't been that long since they were referred to as "police women" and the change was affecting a lot of people in different ways. Some of the male officers were supportive of their female counterparts; others were not so happy about the change.

During the time I was employed with CPD, I had several conversations with some of my female friends about advancement in the ranks. These women had that combination of street smarts and book knowledge that would have made them excellent leaders. Unfortunately, none of the women I befriended were willing to take the promotional exam because they didn't want to be the first female sergeant. Their reasoning was that whoever went first was going to have a lot of obstacles to overcome and they didn't feel they were up to the challenge. Fortunately, there were other women who were willing to take that leap of faith.

Kimberly Jacobs wasn't the first female sergeant (Mary Lester holds that distinction), but she was one of the first two sergeants promoted to lieutenant. She continued her rise through the ranks to become the first female commander, and in 2009 Ms. Jacobs became the first female deputy chief in the Columbus Police Department's 193 year history. Who knows what other ceilings she will shatter?

Somebody has to go first to clear the path for others. So, ask yourself this question: Is there anything God is asking you to do that would pave the way for someone else? If there is, then you need to get busy!

THE REST OF THE STORY

Remember I stated earlier in this chapter that God is just waiting for us to ask the right question, in the right way, so that He is then freed up to work on our behalf? Well, ap-

71

proximately a year after Mahlah, Noah, Hoglah, Milcah and Tirzah's request had been granted, some of their relatives took a page from their boldness and went to Moses with their own request:

> *When the Lord commanded my lord to give the land as an inheritance to the Israelites by lot, he ordered you to give the inheritance of our brother Zelophehad to his daughters. Now suppose they marry men from other Israelite tribes; then their inheritance will be taken from our ancestral inheritance and added to that of the tribe they marry into. And so part of the inheritance allotted to us will be taken away* (Numbers 36:2-3, NIV).

You can't blame the family for wanting to keep their inheritance among themselves, which is why when Moses took their petition before the Lord it was met with favor:

> *This is what the Lord commands for Zelophehad's daughters: They may marry anyone they please as long as they marry within the tribal clan of their father. No inheritance in Israel is to pass from tribe to tribe, for every Israelite shall keep the tribal land inherited from their forefathers. Every daughter who inherits land in any Israelite tribe must marry someone in her father's tribal clan, so that every Israelite will possess the inheritance of his fathers. No inheritance may pass from tribe to tribe, for each Israelite tribe is to keep the land it inherits* (Numbers 36: 6-9, NIV).

Since it was never the sisters' intention to be rebellious— they just wanted what they believed belonged to them—they had no problem agreeing with God's command. They mar-

Chapter Six — Sisters On A Mission

ried cousins on their father side and their inheritance remained within the tribe (Numbers 36:10-11). But none of this would have happened if they hadn't taken the initial step of coming into agreement.

What would it take for you to put aside your preference, your opinion or your ego to achieve something long-lasting?

Chapter Seven —
So Much To Do, So Little Time

As a Type II diabetic, every three months I have to endure what I call the big blood test. This is where my doctor's nurse pretends to be a vampire and tries to suck all of the blood from my body by taking tube after tube after tube of the red stuff. I am fortunate in that my doctor uses an excellent lab and the results are usually available the following day. However, during the waiting period, I am filled with both dread and excitement. I feel dread because I am anxious to know whether anything has changed with my diabetes which would result in a change in my medicine. I feel excitement because I am anxious to know whether anything has changed with my diabetes which would eliminate some of the prescribed medication.

Now if I feel like that waiting for test results, I can only imagine what the children of Israel felt coming to the end of their forty-year journey with the reality of inhabiting the Promised Land becoming more real with every step.

THE JORDAN RIVER EXPERIENCE

What is the best way to repay someone for a job well done? Drum roll please...give them another job!

Joshua had been with Moses throughout the exodus from Egypt, the parting of the Red Sea, the appointment of elders, the backstabbing of family members and the frustration and disillusionment of dealing with obstinate people. Joshua had demonstrated himself to be a leader instead of a follower when he and Caleb brought back the only positive report about the Promised Land. They were willing to go against the other ten spies and pointed out the potential for inhabiting the land despite what their eyes saw. Yes, there were giants. Yes, the cities were fortified. And yes, there were going to be obstacles to overcome. But Joshua and Caleb had faith enough to believe that the God who had brought them thus far was well able to take them the rest of the way. And as a result of his faithfulness, Joshua was publicly endorsed by Moses as the apparent heir:

> *Then Moses summoned Joshua. He said to him with all Israel watching, "Be strong. Take courage. You will enter the land with this people, this land that God promised their ancestors that He'd give them. You will make them the proud possessors of it. God is striding ahead of you. He's right there with you. He won't let you down; He won't leave you. Don't be intimidated. Don't worry"* (Deuteronomy 31:7-8, The Message).

And God co-signed Moses' endorsement:

> *God spoke to Moses: You are about to die. So call Joshua. Meet me in the Tent of Meeting so that I can commission him...Then God commanded Joshua son of Nun saying: "Be strong. Take courage. You will lead the People of Israel into the land I promised to give them. And I'll be right there with you"* (Deuteronomy 31:14, 23, The Message).

The Promised Land was closer than it had ever been, but before the Israelites could embrace their destiny they had to cross the Jordan River. Some of the women getting ready to cross the Jordan River had also crossed the Red Sea with Moses—all of the men twenty years and older had been killed in the wilderness because of rebellion (Numbers 14:1-45)—but this would be a new experience for most of the Israelites. Yet, they willingly followed Joshua, who bore God and Moses' stamp of approval, because he could help them

Chapter Seven — So Much To Do, So Little Time

obtain their inheritance. Both Moses and God repeatedly assured Joshua that he was equipped to handle the responsibility bestowed upon him, he wasn't alone and he would be successful:

> *Moses my servant is dead. Get going. Cross this Jordan River, you and all the people. Cross to the country I'm giving to the People of Israel. I'm giving you every square inch of the land you set your foot on, just as I promised Moses...All your life, no one will be able to hold out against you. In the same way I was with Moses, I'll be with you. I won't give up on you; I won't leave you. Strength! Courage! You are going to lead this people to inherit the land that I promised to give their ancestors* (Joshua 1:2-3, 5-9, The Message).

If asked, most people would be able to tell you where they were and what they were doing on September 11, 2001. I happened to be in a plane on my way to a small group conference in New Orleans with four of my fellow church members. We had a scheduled stop in Atlanta, Georgia and were unaware of what had happened until we were almost ready to land. There was something in the captain's voice when he said, "Ladies and Gentlemen, may I have your attention" that caught my ear. Perhaps it was the fact that he paused before continuing, or perhaps it was the somberness and seriousness of his voice. I wasn't sure what he was getting ready to announce, but I knew it didn't have anything to do with our plane malfunctioning or anything like that. But even if I could have imagined what the captain was about to say, I would never have imagined correctly. Who could?

When the captain began speaking again, he provided a brief explanation of what had happened, and then proceeded to assure us that we were going to land safely in

77

Atlanta. He told us the airport was being evacuated and we would be instructed where to go to get transportation. He emphasized that it was important to proceed quickly, but safely, through the terminal. As we were making that long walk from the plane to the transportation trains some of my fellow passengers were pausing at exhibits and looking in storefront windows as if they were on vacation! I couldn't believe it. My only focus was on getting through the terminal as quickly as possible. The Atlanta airport is one the busiest in the country, but that day it was virtually deserted and eerily quiet, and I couldn't get out of there quick enough!

I would imagine that some of the people crossing over a dry Jordan River had a similar sense of urgency. They had business to take care of and in order to do that they had to get to the other side. They crossed the Jordan River without dawdling and everyone passed over without incident. No one was lost and no one got wet!

> *Now the Jordan is at flood stage all during harvest. Yet as soon as the priests who carried the ark reached the Jordan and their feet touched the water's edge, the water from upstream stopped flowing. It piled up in a heap a great distance away, at a town called Adam in the vicinity of Zarethan, while the water flowing down to the Sea of the Arabah (the Salt Sea) was completely cut off. So the people crossed over opposite Jericho* (Joshua 3:15-16, NIV).

Joshua led the children of Israel across the Jordan River and into their future. Little did he know that shortly after reaching the other side of the river he would come to understand first-hand one of life's greatest ironies: You can be high on the mountain today and low in the valley tomorrow.

Chapter Seven — So Much To Do, So Little Time

THE JERICHO SUCCESS

When Joshua told the children of Israel how they were going to overcome the city of Jericho, I am convinced that some of them thought that Moses had made a serious mistake by putting him in charge! Although his plan of attack was very unusual, they were still willing to follow his instructions:

> *March around the city once with all the armed men. Do this for six days. Have seven priests carry trumpets of rams' horns in front of the ark. On the seventh day, march around the city seven times, with the priests blowing the trumpets. When you hear them sound a long blast on the trumpets, have all the people give a loud shout; then the wall of the city will collapse and the people will go up, every man straight in...Do not give a war cry, do not raise your voices, do not say a word until the day I tell you to shout. Then shout!* (Joshua 6:3-5; 10, NIV).

Joshua had to have confidently planned for the destruction of Jericho. After all, God had assured him that he would be successful—*"You are going to lead this people to inherit the land that I promised to give their ancestors"* (Joshua 1:6)— and being a mighty man of faith, he planned for the destruction of Jericho accordingly. As the children of Israel most likely discovered, being obedient to God's instructions isn't always easy. Being told to march around a city for six days in total silence had to be challenging, and I am always surprised that they actually did it.

Just about every Sunday at some point during the sermon my pastor will say something like, "Everybody say such and such," at which time some of the people respond correctly, but more often than not you will also hear, "Praise the Lord," or "Hallelujah," or "Amen," or people

79

clapping their hands. While these acts of worship are certainly appropriate, my pastor's instruction was for everybody to say the designated phrase. Whenever this happens I always have the same thought: If my pastor can't get a few thousand people to agree to do the same thing, how in the world did Joshua get well over a million people (601,730 men plus women and children according to Numbers 26:51) to be obedient?

I think it was because they wanted their land, and if they had to be quiet to get it, then that is what they were going to do. They realized it wasn't about individual needs; they were going to inherit as a people and everyone had to do their part to ensure that happened. I would imagine that even when they wanted to say something, they remained silent because the consequences of talking were too great to risk.

For six days the Israelites quietly walked around Jericho; on the seventh day they gave a great shout and once again saw God move on their behalf when the walls fell down. Unfortunately, the sweet taste of victory would soon turn sour.

SOMETIMES YOU JUST HAVE TO SHUT UP!

Years ago a friend of mine began dating a former boyfriend and the day I met him resulted in one of the more unusual instances of God speaking to me. We were sitting in her living room having one of those getting-to-know-you conversations. The subject of children came up and I discovered that he had a daughter who he was estranged from because she had two children out of wedlock by two different men. He went on and on about how inappropriate that was and why he didn't have anything to do with his daughter. Now what was interesting to me about this dialogue was that my friend was in the exact same situation: An unmarried with two children by two different men. After several minutes of listening to him spout nonsense, I had heard enough. I

Chapter Seven — So Much To Do, So Little Time

actually opened my mouth to point out the obvious double standard of his statements, but before the words could even begin to form, I clearly heard the Holy Spirit say, "SHUT UP!!!" in capital letters with exclamation points. I had never heard God speak in such a forceful way. I know that if either of the other two people in the room had been looking at me instead of each other they would have literally seen my mouth snap shut, and because I could imagine what I looked like, I started to chuckle. They, of course, wanted to know what was so funny but I couldn't tell them.

Later that evening I asked God why He had done that and He told me He had to grab my attention quick before I said something that would have destroyed the relationship with my friend, and He assured me He would take care of things. Months later, as my friend's relationship became more serious, I was able to talk with her about what had happened. She confessed that she had picked up on the same vibe that I had, and couldn't figure out his statements since he knew about her children. As time went on, she was able to speak with her future husband about it, which resulted in him and his daughter's relationship getting better.

The moral of this story is that the Creator of the universe doesn't really need our help to get things done. Sometimes you just have to shut up so that God can work things out the way He wants to without our butting in. I know the children of Israel would agree.

WHAT HAPPENS WHEN YOU'RE CAUGHT IN THE MIDDLE?

Achieving victory on your first venture will usually inspire you to keep going. The defeat of Jericho was successful; there was no reason for Joshua to think that the battle with Ai would be different. He entered Ai fully confident that another victory was his, but he was in for a very big surprise. During the destruction of Jericho, Joshua had told the children of Israel to:

> *Destroy with the sword every living thing in it—men and women, young and old, cattle, sheep and donkeys* (Joshua 6:21, NIV).

That was the plan, and like what often happens, someone believed that the rules didn't apply to them and that they wouldn't get caught. One of Joshua's men, Achan, decided to keep some of the devoted things for himself:

> *Then they burned the whole city and everything in it, but they put the silver and gold and the articles of bronze and iron into the treasury of the Lord's house* (Joshua 6:24, NIV).

An important point in the story is to remember that Achan stole for himself, not for his family, or like king Saul who pretended that the things he took were for God (I Samuel 15:12-24). Achan saw something he wanted and his greed overrode his common sense. He had no inkling that the ramifications of his disobedience would be so deadly:

> *Go up and spy out the region...when they returned to Joshua, they said, "Not all the people will have to go up against Ai. Send two or three thousand men to take it and do not weary all the people, for only a few men are there." So about three thousand men went up; but they were routed by the men of Ai, who killed about thirty-six of them. They chased the Israelites from the city gate as far as the stone quarries and struck them down on the slopes. At this the hearts of the people melted and became like water* (Joshua 7:2-5, NIV).

Chapter Seven — So Much To Do, So Little Time

After this unexpected defeat, Joshua tore his clothes, fell on his face and spent a significant amount of time mourning his fate. God finally got sick of his whining:

> *Stand up! What are you doing down on your face? Israel has sinned; they have violated my covenant which I commanded them to keep. They have taken some of the devoted things; they have stolen, they have lied, they have put them with their own possessions. That is why the Israelites cannot stand against their enemies; they turn their backs and run because they have been made liable to destruction. I will not be with you anymore unless you destroy whatever among you is devoted to destruction* (Joshua 7:10-12, NIV).

Joshua took a survey of the camp and eventually identified Achan (who had stubbornly refused to come forward) as the culprit. Achan admitted to the theft of a beautiful robe, two hundred shekels of silver and a wedge of gold weighing fifty shekels (Joshua 7:21). He told them where the items were hidden in his tent. Unfortunately, Achan's actions didn't just affect him since he, his wife and children were stoned, and all of them, their possessions and the stolen items were burned. This story illustrates the deadly consequences of doing your own thing. Achan didn't discuss any of this with his wife; yet his entire family was sacrificed because of his greed and disobedience.

Notice that this chapter emphasizes two aspects of agreement. The children of Israel forged together as a group to believe in and agree with their leader. As a result of their obedience they were able to experience something both great and miraculous. On the other hand, Achan agreed with himself to steal something that didn't belong to him. Unfortunately his disobedience led to the demise of himself and his family. Both of these examples remind us that everything we do affects someone else.

Chapter Eight —
Let's Give A Shout Out To Forest Gump

My grandsons love to play with those flexible hand-held action figures that are about three or four inches tall. Whenever they come in town they rush to show me their latest favorite toy, which changes from visit to visit and day to day. One time the green man is their favorite and they carry him around all day. The next day the military man is the new favorite.

A lot of adults are like my grandsons. Today their "must-have" toy is one thing; tomorrow it will be something else. And what they just absolutely, positively couldn't live without a few months ago no longer hold their interest. If anyone could ever figure out the fickleness of people, they would become a gazillionaire!

One of the saddest stories in the Bible involves a young man whose fickleness caused the destruction of his family. A spoiled prince named Amnon, the eldest son of Israel's most beloved king, believed that he could have whatever he wanted, whenever he wanted it and from whomever he wanted, and he became obsessed with the one woman he should have left alone: *"Do not have sexual relationships with the daughter of your father's wife, born to your father; she is your sister"* (Leviticus 18:11, NIV). Because of Amnon's sense of entitlement and lack of discipline, four lives were destroyed: his own; his brother, Absalom; his sister, Tamar; and his father, David. And the real tragedy is that all of this could have been avoided.

FROM OBSESSION TO POSSESSION

"Between love and madness lies Obsession" may be a provocative tag line for Calvin Klein's Obsession perfume, but it makes a deplorable reality. Anytime you focus on something

so intently you are bound to become obsessed, which is not necessarily a bad thing unless you take it to the extreme.

King David had a lot of wives and a lot of children. Among them was his eldest son Amnon, born to his wife Ahinoam, and his third son Absalom and daughter Tamar, born to his wife Maacah: *"In the course of time, Amnon son of David fell in love with Tamar, the beautiful sister of Absalom son of David"* (2 Samuel 13:1, NIV). We are not told how old these three are at the time of this incident or how long Amnon had been waiting and wanting to be intimate with his sister. But we do know that he watched her constantly, thought about her incessantly, lusted after her continuously and made himself sick!

STUPID IS AS STUPID DOES

One definition of the word "stupid" is acting in an unintelligent or careless manner. No two people fit this definition better than Amnon and his cousin, Jonadab. When Amnon began to look haggard and depressed because of his obsession with his sister, Jonadab noticed his behavior and asked about the cause. Amnon confessed that he was in love with his sister, and instead of Jonadab pointing out the inappropriateness of this feeling, he immediately concocted a scheme to give Amnon what he wanted.

Amnon and Jonadab weren't just cousins; they were friends, although Jonadab proved himself not to be very good at the friendship thing. A true friend would have pointed out to Amnon that he could have any woman he wanted and to find someone else. Because of the ease of the suggestion and acceptance of the plan, I am inclined to believe that perhaps Jonadab and Amnon had pulled this act before on other unsuspecting women. They were able to read each other well and both knew how the story was going to end:

Chapter Eight — Let's Give A Shout Out To Forest Gump

> *"Go to bed and pretend to be ill,"* Jonadab said. *"When your father comes to see you, say to him, 'I would like my sister Tamar to come and give me something to eat. Let her prepare the food in my sight so I may watch her and then eat it from her hand'"* (2 Samuel 13:5, NIV).

A request for food isn't that unusual since preparing food for sick people is part of the unofficial healing process. And even the request for Tamar to prepare it wasn't out of the ordinary. It is possible that although she was a princess she had a fondness for cooking, and it is also possible that she had prepared this particular meal for her family before. There are certain people who can prepare certain foods in a certain way that makes the eating experience memorable. (I can still remember my mother's meatloaf and my paternal grandmother's fried chicken, and both of them have been in heaven more years than I care to remember). What was uncharacteristic about this request was the profound deviousness behind it. Tamar was a virgin; she didn't know how to recognize lust from a man, and even if she had, she wouldn't have expected it from her brother.

There was nothing unusual about Amnon watching his unsuspecting sister preparing his meal. What was unusual was that he knew what was going to happen once the food was ready. He asked her to bring the prepared dish to his bedroom where he grabbed her and told her to get into bed. She resisted and pointed out that he could speak to the king who would give him to her. (I think the only reason she made that offer was to deter Amnon; she knew the law prevented them from getting married, Leviticus 20:17). Whatever the reason for the statement, it didn't stop Amnon from the path he had decided to take:

> *But he refused to listen to her, and since he was stronger than she, he raped her. Then*

Amnon hated her with intense hatred. In fact, he hated her more than he had loved her. Amnon said to her, "Get up and get out!" (2 Samuel 13:14-15, NIV).

Tamar begged her brother not to discard her, but he did it anyway:

He called his personal servant and said, "Get this woman out of here and bolt the door after her." So his servant put her out and bolted the door after her. She was wearing a richly ornamented robe, for this was the kind of garment the virgin daughters of the king wore. Tamar put ashes on her head and tore the ornamented robe she was wearing. She put her hand on her head and went away, weeping aloud as she went (2 Samuel 13:17-19, NIV).

Two of the most powerful emotions in the world are love and hate, and as is often suggested, there is a thin line between the two. The Bible says Amnon hated Tamar more than he loved her. Perhaps once he had satisfied his urge he no longer had a desire for her, but I think Amnon's hatred stemmed partly from guilt. He knew he was wrong for raping her and then throwing her out. He was disgusted with himself for his actions, mad at Jonadab for co-signing his craziness and mad at himself for being too weak to deny himself. Unbeknownst to Amnon, those illicit moments with Tamar signed his death warrant.

When Absalom saw his sister, Tamar, he asked one question: *"Has that Amnon, your brother, been with you?"* (2 Samuel 13:20(a), NIV). For me, the asking of that question raises some interesting points. Why did he immediately think that Amnon had done something to Tamar? Had he

Chapter Eight — Let's Give A Shout Out To Forest Gump

noticed Amnon's unusual attraction to her? And, if so, why didn't Absalom chastise him for lusting after his sister?

> *"Be quiet now, my sister, he is your brother. Don't take this thing to heart." And Tamar lived in her brother Absalom's house, a desolate woman* (2 Samuel 13:20(b), NIV).

I used to think that Absalom's reaction to what had happened to his sister—*"Don't take this thing to heart"*—was the embodiment of insensitivity until my son started using a similar phrase. He frequently says, "shake it off," which essentially means to deal with what the issue is and then move on; don't stay stuck.

> God, give us the grace to accept with serenity the things that cannot be changed, Courage to change the things which should be changed, And the wisdom to distinguish the one from the other.

The Serenity Prayer, written by Reinhold Niebuhr, is so powerful in its simplicity because it gets right to the heart of what we need to do: When you have done all you can, let it go. There are some things we will never be able to change. Do we regret them? Absolutely, but we can't allow them to eat at us to the point that we can't move on. Having said that, I do realize that sometimes shaking things off (or not taking things to heart) is easier said than done, and some things are easier to shake off than others.

AFTERSHOCKS

Tamar was a virgin when she entered Amnon's bedroom and a fallen woman when she left. She had been used and discarded by her brother who gave no more thought to Tamar's feelings than he would to stepping on a bug. Her brother, Absalom, took her into his house but told her not to dwell on her feelings. Her father totally ignored what his favorite son had done to her. Is it any wonder she was desolate? Her mind, body and spirit had been broken by what Amnon did. He didn't just rape her physically; he destroyed her psyche. She expected to remain a virgin until she married; he had taken the one gift that can't be repackaged away from her. She would never marry. She would never bear children. She would be alone for the rest of her life. Tamar was never able to recover from the trauma and disappointment of being used and discarded like trash and, unlike her brother's suggestion, she couldn't help but take what had happened to heart.

Although what Amnon did was despicable, what David did was worse. Why didn't he defend his daughter? He might not have been expecting to confront evil in his own home, but David was a warrior. He had fought lions, bears and Goliath; enemies, Saul and his own lusts, so why didn't he fight for Tamar? The Bible says he was furious when he heard about this incident, but it gives no indication that David ever spoke with Amnon about his behavior. David doted on Amnon and was upset at what had happened, but not upset enough to do anything about it. His inaction set in motion events that would lead to one son's death and the other son's estrangement, as well as a daughter who would never recover emotionally from what had been done to her. The Bible records no interaction between father and daughter, but what could David possibly have said to Tamar to justify his lack of concern?

While Absalom may not have been the most tactful person Tamar could have run into immediately following the rape, he did have one trait that evidently had been well hidden: Patience. On the surface he appeared to be at peace with the rape, but then he patiently plotted and planned for two years before avenging his sister and striking back at his father for not doing anything about it. After killing Amnon, Absalom fled to Geshur, his grandfather's country, where he

Chapter Eight — Let's Give A Shout Out To Forest Gump

would live for three years. He eventually returned to Jerusalem, but he and David's relationship would never be the same.

Interestingly enough, the culprit of this whole mess—Jonadab—appears to have gotten away unscathed. He was the instigator of the plot to destroy Tamar, although it probably wasn't intentional. I don't think Jonadab gave any thought to how Tamar was going to react, and I am positive he didn't plan on Amnon getting killed. He was only trying to help his friend and cousin, instead of taking time to look at the bigger picture. I often wonder if he had any remorse for the part he played in this fiasco. There are some commentators who believe that he was trying to make amends by hastening to tell David that only Amnon had died and not all of his sons as had erroneously been reported to him (2 Samuel 13:32 (a)), but even if that were Jonadab's motive, this was clearly a case of too little, too late.

This tragic story clearly illustrates that the power of agreement will work whether it is for good or evil.

Chapter Nine —
Evil, Eviler, Evilest

I fell in love with the written word the first time I read *See Spot Run* as a little girl. I like books with characters that are able to bring a wide range of emotions out of me while I am absorbed in their story. I like a good plot with intrigue and drama, humor and suspense. I like a well-written story that keeps me turning the pages until I get to the end. I like the unpredictability of the unexpected. And nowhere is my literary criteria better met than in the Bible. Whether reading the traditional King James Version or a more modern interpretation, the Bible is filled with drama, intrigue, passion, humor, life and death.

One of the reasons I enjoy reading the Bible is because it is filled with stories about all types of people, in all types of circumstances, doing all types of things. The majority of the Bible characters are ordinary people sometimes called to do extraordinary things such as Moses, the Virgin Mary or John the Baptist. However, there are a number of Bible characters who embody the dangerous combination of low morals and serious character flaws. King Ahab and Queen Jezebel were two such people.

DOING WHAT COMES NATURALLY

I truly believe in generational curses as well as generational blessings, and what I know to be true about both curses and blessings is that only you can decide which one you will embrace. Just because something has always been done a certain way doesn't mean it has to continue. The choice is yours as to which road you will travel and what you want to be remembered for when it is all said and done.

Ahab's father, Omri, was evil:

Obieray Rogers

> *But Omri did evil in the eyes of the Lord, even worse than all who were before him. He walked in all the ways of Jeroboam son of Nebat and in his sin, by which he made Israel sin, to provoke the Lord, the God of Israel, to anger with their idols* (I Kings 16:25-26, The Message).

Ahab was eviler:

> *Ahab son of Omri was king over Israel for twenty-two years. He ruled from Samaria. Ahab son of Omri did even more open evil before God than anyone yet — a new champion in evil! It wasn't enough for him to copy the sins of Jeroboam son of Nebat; no, he went all out, first by marrying Jezebel daughter of Ethbaal king of the Sidonians, and then by serving and worshiping the god Baal. He built a temple for Baal in Samaria, and then furnished it with an altar for Baal. Worse, he went on and built a shrine to the sacred whore Asherah. He made the God of Israel angrier than all the previous kings of Israel put together* (I Kings 16:30-33, The Message).

And Ahab's wife was evilest:

> *Ahab, pushed by his wife Jezebel and in open defiance of God, set an all-time record in making big business of evil. He indulged in outrageous obscenities in the world of idols, copying the Amorites whom God had earlier kicked out of Israelite territory* (I King 21:25, The Message).

Chapter Nine — Evil, Eviler, Evilest

Being king wasn't enough for Ahab. He wanted more, and he knew that marrying someone more unscrupulous than he would help him achieve his goal. The evilness of Ahab would take too much time to cover, but I do want to look at one specific instance where by silently agreeing with his wife, Jezebel, and her take-no-prisoners mentality, he allowed her to commit murder.

WAS IT ALL ABOUT THE GRAPES?

I have deduced after several readings of the biblical story of Ahab that he was a very immature individual. He was frequently noted to sulk, which is something children do. He whined whenever he didn't get his way, which is something children do. He wanted things that didn't belong to him, which is something children do. The only adult thing he appears to have done was marry Jezebel and that was probably because someone else arranged it for him!

Ahab coveted a vineyard owned by Naboth of Jezreel because it bordered the palace. To his credit Ahab did offer to buy the property or to trade it for another piece of land, but Naboth didn't want to sell the vineyard because it was a family inheritance. Ahab got mad at the denial, went home, got in bed and refused to eat. When Jezebel came home and discovered his posture, she asked what was wrong. Ahab sniffled and whined and relayed the conversation with Naboth. Jezebel, in typical fashion, cut right to the chase with her response:

> Is this any way for the king of Israel to act? Aren't you the boss? On your feet! Eat! Cheer up! I'll take care of this; I'll get the vineyard of this Naboth the Jezreelite for you (I Kings 21:7, The Message).

Ahab knew his wife and her personality. He knew when he whined to her about Naboth that she would handle things

95

in her usual way. He never bothered to ask how she was going to get the land, but he had to have known it wasn't going to be pleasant for Naboth. After all, he had offered to purchase the land or give him another piece of land in exchange. Since Naboth had already said no to Ahab, there wasn't going to be anything Jezebel could offer him to convince him to part with the property. Ahab knew she was going to do something unethical and illegal, and he didn't even try to stop her.

Jezebel enjoyed power and knew how to wield it. She used Ahab's influence to send out letters to city officials and leaders to hold a fast day and put Naboth at the head table. She arranged for them to have men at the event who would accuse Naboth of blasphemy against God and the king so they could stone him. Once dead, the vineyard would be Ahab's for the taking. Sadly, Jezebel's plan went off without a hitch and Naboth was killed. When she told Ahab that he was dead, Ahab immediately went to the vineyard and claimed it for himself, only to discover that just when you think you have gotten away with something God steps in to remind you of His omniscience. He sent Elijah to confront Ahab about what he had done:

> "Say this to him: 'God's word: what's going on here? First murder, then theft?' Then tell him, 'God's verdict: the very spot were the dogs lapped up Naboth's blood, they'll lap up your blood—that's right, your blood'" (I Kings 21: 19, The Message).

God didn't forget about Jezebel either: *"Dogs will fight over the flesh of Jezebel all over Jezreel"* (I Kings 21:23(a), The Message).

Ahab was so distressed by Elijah's prophecy that he immediately tore his clothes, fasted and repented. God decided not to fulfill the prophecy given to Elijah in Ahab's lifetime, but his son would not be so fortunate (I Kings

Chapter Nine — Evil, Eviler, Evilest

21:21-29). After all his coveting, plotting and scheming, in the end Ahab didn't get to enjoy the vineyard, which made Naboth's death even more senseless.

GOD IS THE MASTER OF THE UNEXPECTED

Sometimes surprises are good, like when you receive a card or gift just because someone was thinking of you. Sometimes surprises are not so good, like when you stick your hand in a child's pocket and pull out something icky. And sometimes surprises are just plain horrible, like being laid off six months before you're eligible for retirement. I recently had a very good surprise from God because it was so totally unexpected.

I personally believe that my grandsons are everything grandchildren are supposed to be: Smart, polite and well-mannered (most times), very comical and typical of most four and seven-year-old healthy, active boys. Unlike some parents, I never pressured my son into having children, and hadn't given a lot of thought to grandchildren at all, but once they arrived I was amazed at my heart's capacity to expand to include them. They are a joy and a delight to me, and I love them very much.

My son, daughter-in-law and grandsons recently moved two hundred miles away to Cleveland, Ohio. I wasn't thrilled about them moving, but since I know there are people whose children and grandchildren live in different states, I wasn't going to complain too much. Columbus and Cleveland aren't that far from each other; I was just spoiled from them living ten minutes away and seeing them on a regular basis. My son and daughter-in-law assured me I would see them often, just not as much, but that wasn't to be. This past winter the weather was pretty severe in the Cleveland area and a lot of scheduled trips had to be postponed. I discovered that talking to my grandsons on the telephone isn't the same as seeing them in person.

97

One disappointing weekend when a visit had to be postponed due to weather and scheduling conflicts, I poured out my heart to the Lord telling him how much I missed seeing the grandkids. I keep a picture of the four of them—my son, daughter-in-law, and grandsons—on my office desk, so every time I looked at it, I said something to the Lord about them.

My church has three Sunday morning services at seven, nine and eleven; I attend the nine and eleven o'clock services. At the nine o'clock service, I usually sit next to a friend of mine. She and her husband have two girls, a teenager and a two-year-old. My friend's husband plays the piano and organ so he is up front with the other musicians; the teenager is usually in youth church and the two-year-old alternates between the nursery and staying with her mother. She is at that temperamental age where you never know whether she wants to be bothered with you or not. On this particular Sunday she was in a friendly mood. She was so loving and sweet and allowed me to hold her. She kept hugging me and smiling and it made my heart light. She reminded me of my youngest grandson. He is not often the huggy type, but when he is in the mood, he can charm the birds out of the trees! I thanked God that even though I couldn't be with my biological grandchildren, He had sent me a substitute.

Then at the eleven o'clock service, directly in my line of vision was a little boy about three or four being held in his father's arms. This child was the spitting image of my oldest grandson. They looked so much alike that I actually rubbed my eyes to make sure I wasn't hallucinating! This little boy and my grandson could have been twins; they had the same features, the same body type and the same coloring. The only thing different was that my grandson was older and taller than this little boy, but otherwise it was like looking at a real-life photograph. I found myself frequently gazing in his direction, while he was totally unaware of what was going on. I smiled when I realized what God had done:

Chapter Nine — Evil, Eviler, Evilest

Even though my grandson couldn't be in town, God still let me "see" him through this other little boy. I had never been aware of seeing this little boy before, but since that day I often see him and his family and I still can't get over how much he and my grandson resemble each other.

There are times when God will do the unexpected just to bless you. That Sunday morning God showed me, once again, that He is the master of creativity when He used two of his smallest creations to make me feel a little less lonely. I will be eternally grateful for His thoughtfulness toward me.

I intentionally included this antidote in this chapter because I didn't want to end it on a negative note with Ahab and Jezebel. Besides, who is any purer than a child? It is important to understand that there are some people in this world who are truly evil, but the Bible is clear: *"...greater is he that is in you, than he that is in the world"* (I John 4:4, KJV).

Chapter Ten —
Clicking Your Heels Three Times And Wishing For Home Only Works In The Movies

I have a confession to make. I love movies, and the 1939 classic, *The Wizard of Oz*, would easily be at the top of any all-time favorite list I would create. As a child I remember watching this movie with my siblings every Thanksgiving. We were captivated with the dancing and singing; the Munchkins and the flying monkeys; and of course, the witch melting at the end was always something to look forward to. It wasn't until years later that I realized that part of the movie was in color and I became even more enchanted. The wonderful brightness of the costumes, the yellow brick road and the intense green of the Emerald City all contributed to what I believe to be one of the greatest movies ever produced. I have had the pleasure of introducing my two grandsons to this movie, and what they call the "witch movie" is now one of their favorites. We sing all of the songs, and they can imitate the Tin Man and the Scarecrow's dance sequences and even the Cowardly Lion's cry. And, of course, the witch melting at the end is always something they look forward to with excitement.

Okay, I have another confession to make. I love music, especially if a piano is the predominant instrument. I have always wanted to learn how to play and I had actually bought a used piano and took lessons over twenty years ago. However, as a single parent, piano lessons were a luxury I couldn't afford and, regrettably, I had to sell the piano to put food on the table and to keep a roof over our heads. I have never stopped desiring to learn to play, and whenever I hear someone playing this beautiful instrument exceptionally well, I admit to being envious. I have said for years that I have always wanted to play the piano and this year as I was voicing this longing yet again I stopped in mid-sentence and asked myself what was stopping me from fulfilling this goal. I decided that nothing was standing in the way of my desire, so I bought a keyboard and found a piano teacher. The lessons have been going well, although it will probably be a few years before I can master my favorite classical piece—*Rachmaninoff's Piano Concerto No. 2 in C Minor, 2nd Movement*—but it is something to strive for. In the meantime, I can play a mean version of *Twinkle, Twinkle Little Star* and *Mary Had a Little Lamb!*

One thing I know to be true is this: You can sit around and wish for something to happen, and you can even voice a desire for something to happen, but it is only when you actually put action to thought that something is going to happen.

THE GOOD NEWS IS THE BAD NEWS WAS WRONG

I was recently channel surfing and caught a preacher on the *Praise the Lord* program on the TBN channel say, "The good news is the bad news was wrong," and I almost jumped out of my seat. I can't give the preacher the proper credit because I don't know his name, but, hopefully, he won't mind me using his line. The reason the statement grabbed my attention is because I thought of how many times we buy into the negative and give up on something without really trying? How many opportunities, encounters or relationships have we missed out on because we believed the bad report instead of the good? What would happen if we took a chance and discovered that things actually worked out better than we could have imagined?

> *Some time later, however, King Ben-hadad of Aram mobilized his entire army and besieged Samaria. As a result there was a great famine in the city...Now there were four men*

Chapter Ten — Clicking Your Heels Three Times And Wishing
For Home Only Works In The Movies

*with leprosy sitting at the entrance of the city
gates. "Why should we sit here waiting to
die?" they asked each other. "We will starve
if we stay here, and we will starve if we go
back into the city. So we might as well go out
and surrender to the Aramean army. If they
let us live, so much the better. But if they kill
us, we would have died anyway"* (2 Kings
6:24-25; 7:3-4, NLT).

These four men might have had leprosy, but there was
obviously nothing wrong with their rational thinking. In
essence what they said was when you're dead, you're dead,
so if we're going to die, let's do it in style! They demonstrate
the importance of not allowing your circumstances to stop
you from taking a chance. They were willing to risk death in
order to prevent death and if they were going to die it was
going to be on their terms.

Once these men made their decision, they waited until evening to creep into the Aramean's camp. Once there,
they discovered the camp was abandoned. They didn't know
that God had caused their footsteps to sound like speeding
chariots, galloping horses and a great army. The only thing
they knew was that the camp was deserted and all of their
enemy's possessions had been left behind. The lepers decided to eat to their heart's content and hide silver, gold and
clothing. Then they had an epiphany and realized that they
couldn't keep this good news to themselves. They went back
to the city gate and told the gatekeeper what had happened
(2 Kings 7:5-11).

THE WORSE THING YOU CAN IMAGINE IS NOT
ALWAYS THE WORST THING THAT CAN HAPPEN

When the gatekeeper told the king what the lepers had
discovered, the king thought it was a trap by the Arameans:

103

"Hear the message from the Lord! This is what the Lord says. By this time tomorrow in the markets of Samaria, five quarts of fine flour will cost only half an ounce of silver, and ten quarts of barley grain will cost only half an ounce of silver." The officer assisting the king said to the man of God, "That couldn't happen even if the Lord opened the windows of heaven!" But Elisha replied, "You will see it happen, but you won't be able to eat any of it!" (2 Kings 7:1-2, NLT).

The king sent people to check the situation out and was told that what the gatekeeper had said was true. Then all of the people rushed to the camp site to partake of the bounty and Elisha's prophecy came true: Flour and barley sold for an ounce of silver. The king sent his assistant to direct traffic at the gate, but he was knocked down and trampled to death as the people rushed out (2 Kings 7:17), which was also part of Elisha's prophecy.

The lepers who were ostracized from the community because of their disease were instrumental in saving their community. However, in spite of their heroics, the lepers were still lepers, because sometimes doing the right thing doesn't change your circumstances. There was no miraculous healing for them. But, hey, since they had been wise enough to hide some of the bounty, at least their begging days were over!

SINCE GOD SAYS YOU CAN, WHY DON'T YOU?

In order to participate in a college commencement ceremony, there are certain classes that must be mastered. I was always a good student because I love to learn; however, one of the most unanticipated classes I had to take was statistics. I had heard horror stories about the challenge of this subject. Intelligent people I knew were taking the class two

Chapter Ten — Clicking Your Heels Three Times And Wishing
For Home Only Works In The Movies

or three times in order to pass, so I wasn't looking forward to weeks of studying a difficult subject. To make matters worse, one of my friends knew the professor I would have and she told me he was a very inflexible instructor who didn't appear to like answering questions from students.

I became more anxious as the class date approached and I was unable to concentrate on anything else. One day I was sitting at my kitchen table trying to read the Word and instead found myself thinking about this upcoming class. I stopped what I was doing and started to talk to God. I began by pointing out to Him (just in case He had forgotten!) that He had made me and given me a fairly good amount of intelligence. I asked Him not to have me take the class more than once. And I also asked for an instructor whose teaching style was conducive to my learning style. This happened *on a Thursday around six o'clock in the evening* and the class was scheduled to begin that Saturday.

Saturday morning as I drove to school, I reminded the Lord of my request. When I arrived in the classroom there was no instructor, which I thought was strange. A few minutes before the class was to begin the door opened and in walked this tall, queenly woman dressed in African attire. She strode to the front of the class and gave us her name and told us she would be our instructor for the duration of the course. One of my classmates asked what had happened to the man who was supposed to teach and this is what she said, *"On Thursday evening around seven o'clock*, I received a phone call from the dean of the math department. She asked me if I would mind taking over for your original instructor who would be unable to teach the course. I checked my schedule and I told the dean yes. So here I am."

Can you believe that? *One hour after I prayed*, this woman received a phone call to teach the statistics class I was going to be in. And you know what else, she was an excellent teacher. She was a math professor from a sister college who had written books on statistics. She told us to

105

not use the assigned book because although it was titled, *Elementary Statistics,* it made the assumption that you knew something about the subject. This woman didn't make that assumption, although from the way she taught you realized that you actually did know quite a bit about statistics. She was a quintessential example of what I believe a teacher is to be. She had the ability to take what she knew and explain it to someone else in a practical manner. It doesn't matter how much a teacher knows if they are unable to teach in a way that students can understand. I passed statistics with an A and will be forever grateful to God for hearing and answering my prayers, and for this teacher agreeing to fill in for a colleague.

The four lepers were wiling to believe the impossible from a practical standpoint. They formed a cohesive group, agreed on a strategy, implemented the strategy and achieved success. Their philosophy should become our philosophy: If you were to step out in faith and take a chance, what is the worse thing that can happen?

Chapter Eleven —
What? Don't Tell Me You Didn't Know That Was Going to Happen

When I began attending culinary school, I was immediately amazed at the machismo of some of the other students. They would do things like take something off the stove or out of the oven without using a towel or pot holders. Or they would chop things up extremely fast and tease each other if they considered them too slow. Or they would rush around the kitchen in unsafe ways. Today's reality cooking shows such as *Top Chef, Chopped* and *The Next Food Network Star* all seem to have contestants with this same mentality which may make for dramatic television, but is very dangerous. I still have the scar from where the spray nozzle on the commercial dishwasher slipped out of my hand and practically took my thumb off, which only proves that even when you are paying attention accidents can still happen.

But there are accidents, and then there are intentional set ups. The third chapter of Daniel tells the dramatic story of three young men of royal birth from Judah who were taken captive when Jerusalem was occupied by Babylon under Nebuchadnezzar II. The king's instructions were clear as to what he wanted:

> "...young men without any physical defect, handsome, showing aptitude for every kind of learning, well informed, quick to unde-stand and qualified to serve in the king's palace. He was to teach them the language and literature of the Babylonians" (Daniel 1:4, NIV).

Daniel (Belteshazzar), Hananiah (Shadrach), Mishael (Meshach) and Azariah (Abednego) were among the young men taken captive. They were allotted a daily portion of the king's food and wine, and were to be trained for three years before being placed into the king's service (Daniel 1:5). Daniel, Shadrach, Meshach and Abednego refused to defile themselves with the king's food and were given permission to eat vegetables and drink water for ten days. At the end of that time they were discovered to be healthier and better nourished than the other captives and God gave them knowledge and understanding beyond reason (Daniel 1:8-17). When the king talked with the four men, they were found to have no equal:

> In every matter of wisdom and understanding about what the king questioned them, he found them ten times better than all the magicians and enchanters in his whole kingdom (Daniel 1:19-20, NIV).

Daniel had also been given the ability to understand visions and dreams (Daniel 1:17(b)) and correctly interpreted a dream for Nebuchadnezzar's. In appreciation, Nebuchadnezzar promoted Daniel to ruler over the entire province of Babylon and put him in charge of all the wise men. Daniel didn't forget about his friends, Shadrach, Meshach and Abednego, and at his request the king appointed them administrators over the province of Babylon (Daniel 1:48).

Nebuchadnezzar decided to have a golden image ninety feet high and nine feet wide constructed with the command that whenever people heard music they were to fall down and worship the image. Whoever didn't obey would be immediately thrown into a fiery furnace. Shadrach, Meshach and Abednego refused and some astrologers told the king that they weren't paying attention to him, serving his gods or worshipping the golden image (Daniel 3:12). The king flew into a rage and ordered the three brought before him:

Chapter Eleven — What? Don't Tell Me You Didn't Know That Was Going to Happen

"Is it true, Shadrach, Meshach and Abednego, that you do not serve my gods or worship the image of gold I have set up? Now when you hear the sound of the horn, flute, zither, lyre, harp, pipes and all kinds of music, if you are ready to fall down and worship the image I made, very good. But if you do not worship it, you will be thrown immediately into a blazing furnace. Then what god will be able to rescue you from my hand?" (Daniel 3:14-15, NIV).

Nebuchadnezzar must have thought he could intimidate the young men and became even more irritated when they didn't respond as he thought they should:

"O Nebuchadnezzar, we do not need to defend ourselves before you in this matter. If we are thrown into the blazing furnace, the God we serve is able to save us from it, and He will rescue us from your hand, O king. But even if He does not, we want you to know, O king, that we will not serve your gods or worship the image of gold you have set up" (Daniel 3:16-18, NIV).

Nebuchadnezzar wasn't happy with their response and allowed his emotions to get the best of him. He ordered the furnace to be heated seven times hotter than usual, and ordered that his mighty men of valor tie up and cast Shadrach, Meshach and Abednego into the furnace. The furnace was so hot that the king's men were killed when they opened the door. Shadrach, Meshach and Abednego fell into the furnace fully clothed and tightly bound. Nebuchadnezzar leapt to his feet in amazement at what had happened and looked into the furnace. He was so astonished at what he saw that he asked those around him:

109

"Weren't there three men that we tied up and threw into the fire?" They replied, "Certainly, O king." He said, "Look! I see four men walking around in the fire, unbound and unharmed, and the fourth looks like a son of the gods" (Daniel 3:24-25, NIV).

Nebuchadnezzar went to the furnace opening and shouted for Shadrach, Meshach and Abednego to come out. Not only did they walk out unbound, but to everyone's further astonishment, the fire hadn't harmed their bodies, their hair or their robes, and there was no smell of smoke on them:

Then Nebuchadnezzar said, "Praise be to the God of Shadrach, Meshach and Abednego, who has sent his angel and rescued his servants! They trusted in him and defied the king's command and were willing to give up their lives rather than serve or worship any god except their own God. Therefore I decree that the people of any nation or language who say anything against the God of Shadrach, Meshach and Abednego be cut into pieces and their houses be turned into piles of rubble, for no other God can save in this way." Then the king promoted Shadrach, Meshach and Abednego in the province of Babylon (Daniel 3:28-30, NIV).

Now that's incredible!

CHOOSING WHETHER TO REACT OR RESPOND WILL DETERMINE YOUR ENTERTAINMENT VALUE

Just as Nebuchadnezzar thought that watching Shadrach, Meshach and Abednego burn in the furnace would provide his nightly entertainment, there are people in our lives that

Chapter Eleven — What? Don't Tell Me You Didn't Know That Was Going to Happen

do the same thing. They know exactly which buttons to push to get the reactions they want. When you catch on to what they are doing, they will then change their tactics, but ultimately their goal is the same: They want to watch you explode. A friend of mine told me a true story that perfectly illustrates this point.

My friend and several of her co-workers received an e-mail from their boss describing a new procedure that was to immediately take place that their boss and a third party had discussed. The problem with the information in the e-mail was that my friend knew there were several inaccurate statements within the message. She hit "reply all," pointed out the inaccuracies, and noted how part of the new procedures would backfire because the third party was notorious for not responding to e-mails, answering his telephone or listening to voice mail messages. Since the proposed procedures would affect hundreds of employees, not getting an immediate answer would cause numerous problems that would ultimately somehow become my friend's fault. When the boss read the reply, he hit "reply all" and included the third party with instructions for him to read my friend's response. The boss had sent the e-mail to the third party under the guise of needing clarification, but the real reason for including the third party was to get a reaction. He expected the third party to go ballistic and fire off a nasty e-mail and then expected my friend to respond in kind, but his plan boomeranged.

When my friend realized what had happened, her immediate response was to question her boss, but she said she felt compelled to pray instead. She said that after asking God to take care of the potential mess, she felt at peace. When the co-workers who had been included in the e-mail chain stopped by her office to point out that their boss, in today's vernacular had thrown her under the bus, she assured them the situation would be handled but didn't go into detail. Even when her boss stopped by her office under a pretense of looking for a report she had already sent him, she didn't respond as expected. He wanted her to question his including the third party in the e-mail, but she refused to give him that satisfaction. She gave him the information he pretended to need and since he couldn't get the response he wanted, he left her office.

Several hours later the third party responded to the e-mail and pointed out that what my friend had said was correct, and implicated the boss in deliberately misunderstanding what they had originally talked about and decided upon. My friend believes that because she prayed for guidance, and then allowed God to work things out, she and the third party cancelled the performance her boss thought he was going to see that day. The boss was the only one who came out of the situation looking bad.

The next time you are in a potentially negative situation where you have the choice of responding or reacting, I hope you will do like my friend and refuse to provide the entertainment for people who haven't paid the price of admission.

Chapter Twelve —
Ain't You Got No Home Trainin'?

One definition of a "parent" is one who begets or brings forth offspring, or a person who brings up and cares for another. Now, just in case you don't remember Biology 101, when the male's sperm meets the female's egg, life is created. However, nowhere in this process are you given the choice of which sperm or which egg is going to create you. God chooses the parents He wants us to have, although we may or may not always agree with His choice. He gives us the parents we need to get us to where He wants us to go. Some parents are great; some are good and some are just plain lousy, but I believe that God puts them in our path so that we will develop into what He wants.

Whether you are fortunate enough to have loving parents, or challenged by parents who weren't quite what you would have chosen, only you can decide what you will do with your childhood experiences. If your experiences were great, will you repeat them with your offspring? If your experiences weren't so great, will you wallow in a negative upbringing? Or will you use those negative experiences as a springboard to greatness? I love watching my son interact with his children, because he does a good job with them despite not having a lot of positive male influence during his early years. He and my daughter-in-law are good parents, and I am sure that my grandsons will have fond memories of a wonderful childhood.

My father was a big man, well over six feet tall, with a deep booming voice. He had a very forceful personality which didn't allow for a lot of discussion. When he said jump, you jumped. Because his personality was so domineering, he overshadowed my mother. My mother was a very calm and peaceful person, and I wish I had received more of my personality from her instead of my father. I can honestly say that I do not recall my mother ever raising her voice and she never spanked me. However, there was a time when I knew I had let her down. I cannot remember what I did or said; I can only remember my mother softly saying, "I know you know better." I felt about two inches tall and would have willingly taken a spanking to remove the look of disappointment on her face.

ATTITUDE IS EVERYTHING

Whether you were raised by biological parents, foster parents, adopted parents or an extended family member, all of us have been exposed to some form of manners, whether good or bad. One of the first phrases we teach our children is "thank you," yet it is also one of the first phrases we neglect to use as an adult. It's almost as if some adults believe that they have exceeded their quota for expressing thanks, but the Bible tells us to, *"...give thanks in all circumstances"* (I Thessalonians 5:18, NIV). So that means when you are running late and catch all the green lights, give thanks. When you are unprepared for a presentation and God allows you to look good anyway, give thanks. When you wait until the last minute and still manage to get to work with time to spare, give thanks!

I have chosen to intentionally practice the art of thanksgiving. When I wake every morning on time, and without benefit of an alarm clock, I say thank you Lord, even when I would like to sleep another hour. When I can put my feet on the floor and stand up, I say thank you Lord, because there was a time when I couldn't do it without help. When I can decide what clothes to wear, what to eat or where to go, I say thank you Lord, because things weren't always as good as they are now.

Thankfulness is contagious. If you express thanks to someone, they will usually respond in a positive way, because everybody wants to be appreciated.

Chapter Twelve — Ain't You Got No Home Trainin'?

YOU'LL NEVER RECEIVE HELP IF YOU WON'T OPEN YOUR MOUTH AND ASK FOR IT

Shortly after my youngest grandson started walking he loved to climb onto my bed like he saw his older brother do. He would put his foot on the frame and try to hoist himself up. Unfortunately, he was trying to do this with short, stubby legs and too much behind, but he was persistent. I would watch him to make sure he didn't hurt himself, but I would let him try to do it on his own. Sometimes it took several attempts before he became frustrated enough to ask for assistance. Then he would hold his hand out to me and say, "Help" at which time I extended my hand to give him the leverage he needed to make it to the bed. After a while his legs grew longer and less stubby and he lost the extra padding of a diaper and was able to get himself to the top of the bed without a problem. But sometimes I miss him holding out his hand and asking for help.

I feel that God is like that too. He allows us to try to do things on our own, but sometimes He is waiting for us to hold out our hand to Him and say, "Help."

BEING DIFFERENT ISN'T ALL IT'S CRACKED UP TO BE

In today's pop culture, you have an abundance of entertainers who go out of their way to be different. Everyone wants to think they are a unique trendsetter, but some people have gotten so off course that they have become more freak than fashionista. These people have made a conscious choice to be different in an attempt to stand out in a crowd. But, there are times when the choice of being different has been taken out of our hands.

The seventeenth chapter of the book of Luke tells the story of ten lepers. Lepers were those people who were required to live outside the fringe of society among other lepers because of an infectious skin disease. They were repulsive to look at and were labeled unclean, and anyone

115

who touched them was also considered unclean. The thirteenth and fourteenth chapters of the book of Leviticus provide a thorough explanation of infectious diseases and the extensive process required to be declared clean by the priests. Although lepers were rejected by society, most of them made their living by begging:

> *When He was on the way to Jerusalem, He was passing between Samaria and Galilee. As He entered a village, ten leprous men who stood at a distance met Him; and they raised their voices, saying, "Jesus, Master, have mercy on us!" When He saw them, He said to them, "Go and show yourselves to the priests." (Luke 17:11-14(a), NASB).*

I think it is important to note that Jesus never touched these men; He only spoke the Word to them and that was enough. Have you ever gone to someone thinking they might be able to help you, only to discover they could *really* help you? These men might have thought of Jesus as a good teacher, and might or might not have believed the miraculous stories being told about Him, but when they asked for a handout they didn't realize they were talking to the One who could give them so much more than food and a few coins. What they received was far better.

WHAT HAPPENED TO YOUR FRIENDS?

All ten of the lepers obeyed Jesus' command to go and show themselves to the priest. Once they were declared clean they would have been able to return to society, restore their livelihood and reconnect with their families. But note that their cleansing didn't happen until they took the first step: *"And as they were going, they were cleansed"* (Luke 17:14(b), NASB). Understandably much is made about the one leper who returned to tell Jesus thank you and we have

Chapter Twelve — Ain't You Got No Home Trainin'?

already discussed the importance of being grateful, but now I want to focus on the other nine lepers for just a moment.

Jesus didn't require or request that they come back to thank Him. He had done what He was going to do and had continued on with His business. However, since one of the men decided to show gratitude, Jesus used this as an opportunity to render a valuable life lesson to those standing around:

> *Then Jesus answered and said, "Were there not ten cleansed? But the nine—where are they? Was no one found who returned to give glory to God, except this foreigner?"* (Luke 17:17-18, NASB).

Jesus' question to the group was rhetorical because He already knew the answer, which is why He didn't wait for their response.

I think these nine lepers represent all of those people who erroneously have a sense of entitlement. You know those people who think that everything they receive is suppose to be theirs to begin with. I bet these nine men were very surprised the next time they saw their friend and realized that he had received more than they did. They received only a cleansing, which in and of itself was a wonderful gift, but they could have had so much more if they had just exhibited a little gratefulness. They didn't realize that nobody has to do anything for you, especially God.

AN ATTITUDE OF GRATITUDE

One leper decided that he didn't care what his fellow lepers did; he was going back to say thanks, and he did it with excitement and enthusiasm:

> *Now one of them, when he saw that he had been healed, turned back, glorifying God with*

a loud voice, and he fell on his face at His feet, giving thanks to Him. And he was a Sa- maritan (Luke 17:15-16, NASB).

Leprosy was a disease that often resulted in the loss of limbs, eyesight, hearing and other physical attributes that we take for granted. We know that while these men might have been lepers they still had their hearing, sight and use of limbs. How else would they have heard Jesus' instructions or saw that they were healed? And we know that the one who returned to thank Jesus was limber enough to fall on his face and worship.

Did their healing appear gradually or did it happen all at once? Did they notice each other's faces becoming clearer and their hands appearing smoother? Did one notice that his joints didn't hurt as much? Were their shoulders becoming straighter and their gaits easier? Did they recognize what was happening to them as they made their way to the priest or did it take a moment to sink in? Were they surprised or scared as they noticed the changes occurring?

I know from personal experience that sometimes any change in your physical condition can take you by surprise, especially if you have lived with the condition for a while. I had my knee replaced a few years ago and prior to the surgery, I learned to endure excruciating pain. If you know of anyone who has experienced this particular surgery, then you know that not only is the surgery very painful, but the rehab is almost as bad. One thing my physical therapist stressed was that if I did my exercises (whether I felt like it or not), my knee would begin to feel better. And that is what happened. There were days when the rehab brought tears to my eyes because the pain was so intense, but a few months after faithfully doing my exercises, I realized that although I wasn't yet pain-free, the pain certainly wasn't at the level it was before surgery. By following the instructions of my physical therapist, I was able to see a change in my physical condition.

Chapter Twelve — Ain't You Got No Home Trainin'?

The ten lepers were able to see a change in their physical condition when they followed Jesus' instructions. Unfortunately, only one of them had enough discernment to realize that what had occurred was a miracle that they didn't deserve, and he wanted to say thank you to the One who had changed his physical, societal and environmental condition. He realized that with the healing came a chance to rejoin society. Because he would no longer be considered an outcast, he would be able to live wherever he wanted. He was no longer confined to a leper colony.

I wonder whether this leper ever made it to the priest, or in his excitement did he forget about the priest to run back to Jesus? Either way, as the Only True Priest, Jesus was able to declare him fit for society. It would have been nice if the others had followed his example, but the one who went back did what he knew to be the right thing and was rewarded for it: *"And He said unto him, Arise, go thy way; thy faith hath made thee whole"* (Luke 17:19, KJV). According to *The Strongest Strong's Exhaustive Concordance of the Bible,* the word "whole" in the Greek is sózó, which means, "to save, rescue; deliver, to heal; by extension: to be in right relationship with God, with the implication that the condition before salvation was one of grave danger or distress."

The grateful leper went back to express appreciation for what the Lord had done for him—healed him of leprosy—only to discover that God had so much more to give him.

This one leper entered into an agreement with himself, and we can learn a valuable lesson from him. Expressing an attitude of gratitude, regardless of what anyone else does or does not do, is always right and it is always rewarded.

Chapter Thirteen — Can I Get A Witness?

Have you ever wondered what inspiration songwriters use when composing? Are they writing from personal experience or just looking for words that rhyme? Do they write the words and then the music, or does the music come first and then the lyrics are created to work within the musical notes? *You Always Hurt the One You Love,* written by Doris Fisher and Allan Roberts has been recorded by a variety of musical artists: "You always hurt the one you love. The one you shouldn't hurt at all."

Have you ever been hurt by someone you love? Hurt to the point that you wondered how you would recover from the devastation? Hurt to the point that you vowed never to be put in a vulnerable place again? Hurt to the point that you considered pulling the covers over your head and never getting out of bed? You are in good company if you said yes, because there is a man in the New Testament who can help you get past the hurt.

Our introduction to a spiritual giant named Joseph is as a young man. We are not given any background information regarding his parents or his childhood, but we know he was old enough to be preparing to take on the role of husband. We also know that his life was about to change forever. When most theologians talk about the birth of Jesus they tend to focus on Mary and the role she played, and rightly so. But I want to look at the role Joseph played in this story. If he hadn't been willing to put his pride aside; not worry about what other people thought or said, and agreed with God's plan for his future, then biblical history as we know it may have been changed forever. Could God have found someone else to step into the role of earthly father for the Son of God? Sure. But aren't you glad that Joseph gives us a practical lesson in embracing our destiny.

I wish the Bible had recorded Mary and Joseph's dialogue as she attempted to explain how she would become pregnant. I would love to have eavesdropped on that conversation, wouldn't you? When you read the story, it seems like Joseph immediately and willingly went along with Mary's pregnancy, although it does say that he thought of putting her aside quietly. I think there was more to it than what is recorded. Joseph was a young man who had been dealt a severe and unexpected blow. He was planning on getting married and then having children; not marrying into a ready-made family. There would have been much discussion and a lot of emotion before reaching a decision. He was a human being, not a saint, and he had the same emotions all humans have. He was hurt, he was angry, he was disappointed and he was disillusioned. And he had to process the information before he could fully accept what was being asked of him. That doesn't make him a bad person; just a human one. Since the Bible is silent on the dialogue, I will just have to use my sanctified imagination. Fortunately, I have got a pretty good one. The following is my interpretation of Luke 1:26-38.

Picture this: Nazareth Over Two Thousand Years Ago

The teenage girl stood in front of the fire watching the flames lick at the piece of wood she had just placed on top of the burning embers. She wasn't a fire bug; she just enjoyed watching a fire because it usually had a soothing effect on her, but not today. Her fiancé was on his way over and she wasn't looking forward to the visit, which was so unlike her. Normally, seeing Joe had her in a heightened sense of anticipation and she ran around flustered until she heard his knock at the door.

Mary had loved Joe for as long as she could remember, even though he was older and had totally ignored her until about three years ago. She wasn't sure what happened to change his attitude toward her, but she wasn't going to

Chapter Thirteen — Can I Get A Witness?

question fate. He was the handsomest man she knew. He was tall and broad shouldered, and had a smile that melted her heart every time she saw it. She was so happy when he sought her parents' permission to court her, and thrilled when they said yes. Her father told her Joe was a good choice for a husband. Her parents had known him since he was a child and both sets of parents socialized on a regular basis.

Their wedding was scheduled to take place three months from now. Mary, her mother and her future mother-in-law began planning the celebration the day after Joe proposed. Mary had a good relationship with Joe's mother and she wondered if that was about to change.

Mary smoothed her dress down and took calming breaths. Her hands were damp and her heart was beating too fast. Joe would arrive momentarily and she didn't know if this would be the last time she saw him. She honestly didn't know how she would react if it was, because he was the man of her dreams.

The soft tap at the door drew Mary from her introspection. Her beloved had arrived, but she was hesitant to open the door. The love she felt for him was unlike anything she had ever known, and she knew that she was loved in return. Yet, she hesitated because she knew that once she shared her good news, he might not feel quite the same way about her again. A second, more persistent knock mobilized her into action. "Hi, Joe. Come on in."

"Hey, Mary. How are you today?"

"I'm doing pretty good. Have a seat and let me get you something cool to drink." Mary walked across the room to pour water from the bucket into a cup. As she was making her way back to where Joseph sat, the cup slipped out of her hand and water spilled everywhere. She gave a cry of dismay and watched the water spread across the floor.

"Mary!" Joseph exclaimed "Are you okay? What's the matter?"

Mary focused on Joseph's voice to calm herself down. "I don't know. The cup just slipped. I guess I'm just being clumsy."

"Come and sit down beside me," he said and patted the cushion on the floor next to him. "Are you sure you're okay. You look funny."

"I'm okay. Just sorta tired. I haven't slept well for the last few weeks."

"You're not doing too much are you? I know that you and our mothers have been making plans for the wedding. I can't wait until we're finally married. It's been a long engagement, hasn't it?"

"Uh-huh."

"I've almost got enough money saved to start on our house. It's taken a lot longer than I planned, but I think you'll like what I've designed."

"Uh-huh."

"And then we can start filling the house up with horses and pigs and goats."

"Uh-huh."

"Mary! You're not listening to a word I'm saying. What's the matter with you?"

"Joe...I...oh God, I'm not going to be able to do this." Mary jumped up from the floor and began pacing.

"Not going to be able to do what?" Joseph asked as he, too, stood up. "What's going on?"

"I-I need to tell you something."

"Mary, what's the matter. You know you can tell me anything."

"Something happened and I...See...A few weeks ago I was at home one evening sitting in front of the fire and I heard a sound behind me. I turned around expecting to see Mom or Dad and there was an angel standing in front of me."

"What?"

"An angel who said his name was Gabriel."

"Hmm. An angel named Gabriel came to visit you the other night."

Chapter Thirteen — Can I Get A Witness?

"Uh-huh."

"Why would an angel come to visit you?"

"I asked myself that same question," Mary said as she walked back to where Joseph stood. "I mean I try to keep the commandments and do what's right, but I had never met an angel. Or at least I had never talked to one before. When he appeared he said, 'Greetings, favored woman! The Lord is with you!' and I looked around to see who he was talking to. I realized there was no one in the room except the two of us so I started moving toward the door, but he told me not to be afraid and that God had chosen to bless me."

"Wow, that's deep. Do you think that means God is pleased with our getting married?"

"I hope so. But it gets stranger. After the angel told me not to be afraid, he told me I was going to have a baby. I took that to mean that I wouldn't be barren and we would have a lot of children. You know I've always wanted a large family," Mary said with a wistful smile.

"I know. That's why I work as hard as I do so I can feed everybody," Joseph laughed. "That's great news."

"Uh, Joe, that's not all the angel said."

"There's more? He already told you that God is pleased with you and is going to bless our marriage with children. What else could he have to say?"

"Well, the angel did say that I would become pregnant, but...um..."

"But what? Come on Mary. What else did the angel say?"

"Okay, here goes." Mary paused to take a deep breath and then said in a rush, "The angel said I would have a son and I was to name him Jesus. He would be called the Son of the Most High. He would reign over Israel forever, and his kingdom would have no end."

"Huh. Well, I wanted our first son to be named after me, but I guess I can live with the name Jesus."

"Uh, Joe, that's still not all the angel said."

125

"Look, Mary, this is ridiculous," Joseph said in exasperation. "Just tell me everything the angel told you."

"Are you sure?"

"Of course, I'm sure. Why wouldn't I be? Unless you're getting ready to tell me that the angel wants you to commit murder or something crazy like that, I'm sure I can handle whatever you're getting ready to say." Joseph took Mary's hand, turned her to face him and gentled his voice. "Mary, there's nothing you can say that will ever change the way I feel about you. I love you."

"Oh, Joe, I needed to hear you say that. I love you, too."

"Okay, now tell me what else the angel said."

Mary squeezed Joseph's hand and took another deep breath. She knew that what she was about to say probably wasn't going to be received very well, but he had a right to know what she was getting ready to do. "When the angel talked about the child being great and having a kingdom that would last forever, I didn't think he was talking about you being the father. And before you ask, I don't know why I felt that way. I just did. I asked Gabriel how this was supposed to happen since I was a virgin, and when he answered I knew why I felt strange."

"What did he say, Mary?" Joseph cautiously asked.

"He said that I would be overshadowed by the Holy Spirit so that the baby would be holy. He is to be called the Son of God, not the son of Joseph."

"Excuse me!" Joseph dropped Mary's hand and stepped away from her. "Did I hear you right?"

"Yes, you heard me right. I'm to be impregnated by God and deliver the Messiah. Me. Little Mary from Nazareth. It's too much!" Mary exclaimed and then burst into tears.

"Oh, Mary, don't cry," Joseph said as he reached for her. "Everything's going to be okay. You'll see. Maybe you were just having a dream."

"No, Joe," Mary sniffled. "This wasn't a dream. It was as real as you are right now. I'm going to carry the Messiah."

Chapter Thirteen — Can I Get A Witness?

"What did you tell the angel?"

"I was so stunned by what Gabriel said that I just fell to the ground. I laid there for a while trying to take it all in. When it finally occurred to me exactly what the angel was saying, I began to worship God. And while I was worshipping Him, a strong sense of peace came over me, and I told God that I am His servant and I will do whatever He wants me to."

"Oh, really?" It was Joseph's turn to start pacing. *"What am I supposed to do while you're pregnant? How am I supposed to hold my head up in this community? Our families will think we've slept together. Nobody's going to believe that you're pregnant with God's child."*

"Joe, I know you must be ...."

"No, Mary. I don't think you do know. You don't know what this means." Joseph paused to run his fingers through his shoulder-length hair in a familiar act of frustration. *"What if the child doesn't look like me? Then what? Did you give any thought to how this would affect me, or did you only think of yourself?"*

"Joe, I know you're upset, but please listen to me. Don't you understand? This wasn't just a normal man talking. This was a messenger from God. How was I suppose to tell God no?"

"Well, when you put it like that I guess you couldn't," Joseph sheepishly admitted. *"But do you have any idea what you said yes to?"*

"Not exactly," Mary confessed. *"I just know I couldn't say no, especially when the angel said that my cousin Elizabeth was pregnant, too. She's way older than I am. How could that happen without God's intervention?"* Mary paused to take Joseph's hand again and stare into his eyes. *"Joe, I know this is God's doing. Whether you like it or not, I've agreed to do what God has asked. I'd like to do it with your love and support. Will you stand by me?"*

"I don't know, Mary," Joseph said.

"Are you going to cast me aside?" Mary whispered. "I knew you wouldn't be happy about my news, but I don't want to break our engagement."

"I don't know, Mary," Joseph repeated and released Mary's hand. "I wish we had never had this conversation so things could have stayed the way they are, you know?

"I know," Mary replied.

"Wait a minute. You said this happened a few weeks ago. How many weeks ago?"

"Six weeks ago, yesterday."

"Then why am I just now hearing about it? Why didn't you tell me when you first spoke with the angel?"

"I didn't know how to tell you," Mary confessed.

"Okay, I can see that," Joseph said. "Okay, let me just make sure I understand what you said. An angel visited you and told you God wants you to carry His child and you said yes, is that right?"

"Yes."

"And is his visit the reason you haven't been sleeping well?"

"Yes."

"And when is this miracle supposed to happen?"

Mary caressed her stomach and couldn't prevent a small smile of pleasure from escaping. "It already has."

"So that means..."

"Yes, Joe. I'm carrying the Messiah."

Joseph felt as if his legs could no longer hold him, so he carefully sat back down on the floor. He struggled to get his breath and to wrap his mind about what his fiancée had just told him. She was pregnant with God's child. He shook his head trying to clear his thoughts. "Have you told your parents about this?"

"No, I wanted to talk to you first."

"I appreciate that." Joseph ran his fingers through his hair again and took deep, cleansing breaths. "Mary, I love you and I want to marry you, but you've thrown me for a loop with what you've said. You've given me a lot to think about."

Chapter Thirteen — Can I Get A Witness?

"I understand."

"No, I don't think you do, Mary. I don't think you realize the full magnitude of what you've agreed to and what you're asking me to do. You've had time to process this; I haven't. I need time to think." Joseph stood up and stopped talking. Mary knew he was choosing his words carefully, but wasn't sure she was going to like what he was getting ready to say. "Mary, I don't know what's going to happen, but I will promise you one thing. I will let you know as soon as I decide the best way to handle this. Then we'll go talk to both of our parents. We're either going to tell them that the wedding has been called off, or that the wedding is still on and we're going to have a baby. Either way, I'm sure they'll be just as dumbstruck as I am."

"Okay, Joe," Mary said. "I'll go along with whatever you decide. I love you."

"I love you, too." Joseph placed a whisper of a kiss on Mary's forehead and moved toward the door. "You do realize that life as we've known it has changed forever."

"I know," Mary softly replied. "But this is something I feel I must do."

Joseph was in a precarious position. The entire town knew that he and Mary had been courting and were engaged to be married. The entire town knew, or thought they did, that Mary was a "good girl" and that she would make Joseph an excellent wife. How was he going to explain things to his parents, his friends, his co-workers? He was having a hard time believing what Mary had told him; how could he expect his friends and family to be any different?

THE NEEDS OF THE MANY OUTWEIGH
THE NEEDS OF THE FEW OR THE ONE

Every Trekkie will recognize this phrase from *Star Trek 2: The Wrath of Kahn* which I personally think was the best

Star Trek movie made. The words were spoken to Captain James T. Kirk by his pointy eared friend, Mr. Spock.

There are times when you have to put your feelings aside and look at the big picture. That is not always easy, especially if you have been hurt. What do you do when you think you have been betrayed? Do you confront the betrayer? Do you avoid asking them why? Do you pretend that you are not hurt and try to move on? Or do you remain silent and let things keep festering until you explode?

Have you ever been in a situation that was so baffling that you thought about it constantly with every waking moment spent trying to understand the why of what was going on? Eventually the pondering starts absorbing your sleeping moments too. Joseph was a good man and he wanted to do right by Mary although he was hurt, confused and just downright angry at the circumstances. He carefully considered his options and finally concluded that he had to end the engagement. Obviously our conclusions are not always the way God plans to work things out, but Joseph didn't know that yet:

> *As he considered this, he fell asleep, and an angel of the Lord appeared to him in a dream. "Joseph, son of David," the angel said, "do not be afraid to go ahead with your marriage to Mary. For the child within her has been conceived by the Holy Spirit. And she will have a son, and you are to name him Jesus, for he will save his people from their sins." When Joseph woke up, he did what the angel of the Lord commanded. He brought Mary home to be his wife, but she remained a virgin until her son was born. And Joseph named him Jesus* (Matthew 1:20-25, NLT).

Joseph woke up with a new attitude and clear direction, and did as the angel had instructed.

Chapter Thirteen — Can I Get A Witness?

God wanted an earthly father for Jesus who had a strong moral fiber and good character; a man who would raise His son correctly. God wanted an earthly father for Jesus who would be able to give His son the emotional stability of being raised in a home with an equal portion of love and discipline. God wanted an earthly father for Jesus who would be able to teach His son a skill so he would be gainfully employed. But most of all, God wanted an earthly father for Jesus who would be willing to be used as an example throughout the centuries of how a father takes care of his family.

God knew what He was asking of Joseph when He chose Mary to birth Jesus. He knew that Joseph would struggle with the dilemma, but that once committed he would be the ideal candidate for both Mary's husband and Jesus' earthly father.

YOU'RE ONLY AN INSTRUMENT IN GOD'S TOOL CHEST

When I completed the requirements for my culinary degree, attending commencement was not in my plans. My son was out of state in college and I didn't have the money for him to come home for my graduation. Since the ceremony was in the middle of the day I didn't think any of my family or friends would be willing to take off work just to see me walk across the stage, so I wasn't planning on going. I was focused on the next phase of my education and knew the school would mail me my diploma. This degree was just something to cross off of my "to do" list.

One of my mentors noticed that I hadn't returned the form for my cap and gown and called me into her office. Upon her inquiry I told her that I wasn't going to the ceremony. She sat back in her chair and looked at me, and I patiently waited for her to get to the point. After a few moments, she sat forward in her chair, clasped her hands in front of her and said these words, "You do know that graduation isn't about you, right?" I just looked at her because I

131

wasn't sure where she was going with the conversation. She said, "A lot of times kids want to just blow off walking for graduation because they think it's no big deal. They don't realize that their parents, friends and family want to "see" them walk across the stage. Because you're an older student you probably paid your own way, but still you've invested your time, energy and money. Why not enjoy the entire college experience? I think attending graduation will be something you'll remember for the rest of your life." I told her I would think about it and I left her office.

I seriously considered what my mentor had said and decided to attend the ceremony. On graduation day when the ceremony was over and I was leaving the building to return to work, two remarkable things happened. First, I heard someone call my name and turned to see one of my friends. She had taken an early lunch just to see me graduate. I was glad that she was there even if I didn't know it until after the event. The second thing was that immediately after my friend had spoken to me and left, a woman I had never seen before stopped me. She asked if she could speak with me and I said yes. She said, "I just want you to know that I was inspired seeing you walk across the stage. I've been wondering if maybe I was too old to go back to school—not that I'm saying you're old, because you're certainly not as old as I am—but when I saw you I said, 'Lord, if she can do it, I can, too.' So I just wanted to tell you thanks for helping me make a decision."

What could I say? Once again God showed me that everything we do affects someone else, whether we intend for it to or not. Needless to say, when it came time to graduate with my second degree, I was one of the first students to turn in the form for my cap and gown!

PART THREE

FOREVER. FOR ALWAYS. FOR LOVE.

**Love: Unselfish loyal and benevolent concern
for the good of another.**

Chapter Fourteen — Don't You Want To Know How I Really Feel?

I love you more than anything. Where would I be without your love? Nobody will love you better than me. I was born to love you. My world began the first time you said I love you. I'm only complete with you in my life.

Do any of these phrases sound familiar? They should. If you listen to any love song, you will hear a similar thread running through the lyrics. Why? Because we want to be loved. We want to be admired. We want to be happy. We want to believe that if we just had somebody to love us real good, then everything would be all right. I have nothing against the songwriters who want us to believe that love is the key to happiness; they are entitled to make a living. My dilemma is that the concepts are based on people falling in love, and anytime you fall you are likely to get hurt.

I was invited to a friend's wedding at the church I now attend. Bishop Clarke performed the ceremony and he said something over twenty-five years ago that has stuck with me: Don't fall in love, fall in like. I interpreted that to mean that love will change, but if you have a secure foundation of liking each other you will be able to make it through a lot of difficult times. My pastor understood that people are human and their emotions will change. If you make them happy, they love you; if you irritate them, they can't stand the sight of you. But aren't you glad there is One whose love is unfailing and never changing?

THE MEETING WILL NOW COME TO ORDER

If you ask anyone who the big three of social networking are they would probably say Facebook, LinkedIn and Twitter, depending on who you ask. If you ask anyone who the big three of the car industry are they would probably say General Motors, Ford and Chrysler, depending on who you ask. However, if you ask a Christian who the real big three are they should respond with God, Jesus and the Holy Spirit:

> *In the beginning God created the heavens and the earth. Now the earth was formless and empty, darkness was over the surface of the deep, and the Spirit of God was hovering over the waters. And God said, "Let there be..."* (Genesis 1:1-3(a), NIV).

God spoke into existence day and night, the sky, the sea, trees; sun, moon and stars; water with living creatures, birds flying above the earth and living creatures to move above the ground. As each part of creation was finished, God proclaimed it to be good. But there was one thing left to do:

> *Then God said, "Let us make man in our image, in our likeness, and let them rule over the fish of the sea and the birds of the air, over the livestock, over all the earth, and over all the creatures that move along the ground." So God created man in his own image, in the image of God he created him; male and female he created them. God blessed them and said to them, "Be fruitful and increase in number; fill the earth and subdue it. Rule over the fish of the sea and the birds of the air and over every living creature that moves on the ground"* (Genesis 1:26-28, NIV).

If you have ever studied anatomy, biology or physiology, then you are aware that we are not just skin and bones; we are intricately created:

Chapter Fourteen — Don't You Want To Know How I Really Feel?

...the Lord God formed the man from the dust of the ground and breathed into his nostrils the breath of life, and the man became a living being....but for Adam no suitable helper was found. So the Lord God caused the man to fall into a deep sleep; and while he was sleeping, he took one of the man's ribs and closed up the place with flesh. Then the Lord God made a woman from the rib he had taken out of the man, and he brought her to the man (Genesis 2:7, 19-22, NIV).

In God's mind there was no such thing as a detail too small for His consideration. The ability to blink your eye or to raise a finger; being able to modulate your voice or turn your head from side-to-side; the pointy end of your elbow and the flexing of an ankle are all attributed to the love of God. He could have created us as a big blob, but instead He gave us arms and legs, facial features, chests, waists and knees. We have the ability to hear the slightest sound or the loudest yell; to see the sunrise in the morning and the sunset in the evening; to feel snowflakes and raindrops, as well as the ability to smell the sweet perfume of an orchid and the tantalizing aromas of a home cooked meal.

After God put so much thought into our physical creation, He then focused on our emotions. He provided us with such a wide range because He didn't want us to be one-dimensional. How else could you explain going from tears to laughter in a moment, or expressing the sheer delight of an astonishing surprise? How else can you explain the feelings of love and hate, and having the ability to know the difference? How else can you explain the capacity to experience the pain of sickness, and the elation of feeling well?

The meeting of God, Jesus and the Holy Spirit was called to order to talk about us—you and me—past, present and future.

GUESS WHAT, GRANDMA?

My oldest grandson called me recently with his usual greeting of, "Guess what, Grandma?" He was excited because he had learned to tie his shoes. He talked me through the process and told me that he was very good at tying his shoes and was going to teach his brother. He then asked me if I knew how to tie my shoes, to which I assured him that I had learned that lesson a long time ago. Kids! What are you going to do with them?

My grandsons are at the age where they are constantly changing and learning something new every week as they evolve into the men they will become. They have a sense of wonder and awe with each accomplishment, whether it is learning their ABCs, counting to thirty or tying their shoes, and I hope they never lose it.

It has been a long time since I have learned to recite my ABCs, count to thirty and tie my shoes, but I, too, hope I never lose the sense of wonder and awe at my achievements. I strive to see God's hand in everything, both large and small, and I am always willing to share His accomplishments. I might not call you up and say, "Guess what, Grandma?" but I am very likely to start the conversation with, "You are not going to believe what God did!"

OKAY, I'LL SAY IT FIRST

I have talked with people involved in romantic relationships who were hesitant to express their true feelings because they wanted the other person to express their feelings first. They were reluctant to put themselves in a vulnerable position just in case their feelings weren't reciprocated. God doesn't play that game. He said "I love you" when He

Chapter Fourteen — Don't You Want To Know How I Really
Feel?

created man in His image, so you no longer have to wait for someone else to say it first. You might not feel it or believe it, but it is true. God loves you!

> *You made all the delicate, inner parts of my body and knit me together in my mother's womb. Thank you for making me so wonderfully complex! Your workmanship is marvelous—and how well I know it. You watched me as I was being formed in utter seclusion, as I was woven together in the dark of the womb. You saw me before I was born. Every day of my life was recorded in your book. Every moment was laid out before a single day had passed. How precious are your thoughts about me, O God! They are innumerable! I can't even count them; they outnumber the grains of sand! And when I wake up in the morning you are still with me!* (Psalm 139:13-18, NLT).

Sometimes people say things, and while their intentions are honorable, they can't back up what they say. You can be assured that God isn't like humans. His actions always back up His words. So when I tell you that God says He loves you, you can believe it. In spite of what you are, what you have been or what you are going to become, God loves you!

Unlike the reality show where the man gives a rose to the woman he wants to marry, and then changes his mind after a few months, God is consistent. He is not going to change His mind about how He feels about you.

THE LOVE MULLIGAN

I graduated from high school with a scholarship to a small college in Ohio. It was exciting being away from home for the first time (although I was less than an hour away) and I studied hard and made good grades. However, I wasn't fully persuaded that I needed a degree to find a good job so I left college after two years. Then life happened, and although I tried to avoid the truth for as long as possible, the reality is that for certain positions you actually do need a degree. I returned to college as a forty-year-old woman with a seventeen-year-old son.

I knew that some of my skills were rusty, especially when it came to math, so I opted to take developmental math classes to bring myself up to speed rather than jumping straight into algebra, geometry and calculus. We were given weekly tests and once the tests were returned we were allowed to correct our mistakes for a better grade. The philosophy behind this practice was to ensure that we understood the concept of the problem and the approach necessary to arrive at the correct answer. The instructor believed that putting an incorrect answer down only meant that we had missed a step somewhere in the process.

Anytime an action is repeated because the first attempt wasn't satisfactory, you have done a mulligan. The term is more widely used in golf, but it can also be used in any situation. The meaning behind the word is the chance to do something over, hopefully better.

When God created man and woman, His intention was that they would live forever in the Garden of Eden, interacting with Him on a personal and spiritual level. But, alas, things didn't quite turn out as planned:

> *The Lord God took the man and put him in the Garden of Eden to work it and take care of it. And the Lord God commanded the man, "You are free to eat from any tree in the garden; but you must not eat from the tree of the knowledge of good and evil, for when you eat of it you will surely die"* (Genesis 2:15-17 NIV).

Chapter Fourteen — Don't You Want To Know How I Really Feel?

Adam and Eve allowed a serpent to convince them to disobey God and they ate fruit from the forbidden tree. As a result of their disobedience God banished them from the Garden of Eden. It is important to realize that God could have killed them but chose not to, and because of God's mercy Adam and Eve were allowed to live. They did keep part of the instructions God originally gave them—be fruitful and multiply—and they had three sons: Cain, Abel and Seth. Cain killed Abel in anger and the Lord sent him away from the land as punishment. But, again, God extended mercy; He chose not to kill Cain and put a mark on him so that no one else could kill him either. Adam and Eve's third son, Seth, would have a son named Enosh and, *"It was during his lifetime that people first began to worship the Lord"* (Genesis 4:26, NLT).

> *The Lord saw how great man's wickedness on the earth had become, and that every inclination of the thought of his heart was only evil all the time. The Lord was grieved that he had made man on the earth, and his heart was filled with pain. So the Lord said: "I will wipe mankind, whom I have created, from the face of the earth—men and animals, and creatures that move along the ground, and birds of the air—for I am grieved that I have made them* (Genesis 6:5-7, NIV).

Fortunately for us there was a man who found favor in the eyes of the Lord. Adam's great-great-great-great-great-great-great-great-grandson, Noah, was a *"righteous man, blameless among the people of his time, and he walked with God"* (Genesis 5:3-29; 6:8-9, NIV). From the fall of Adam up to this time man had become increasingly more corrupt and violent, and God had gotten fed up: *"I am going to put an end to all the people, for the earth is filled with violence*

141

because of them. I am surely going to destroy both them and the earth" (Genesis 6:13, NIV). God then told Noah to start building an ark because He was going to flood the earth and everything on it, *"But I will establish my covenant with you, and you will enter the ark—you and your sons, and your wife and your son's wives with you"* (Genesis 6:18, NIV).

What is interesting about this is that not only was God going to create something that up to this point didn't exist—rain—He was only going to save Noah's immediate family. Noah would have over a hundred years to think about the fact that he wouldn't see his brothers and sisters, nieces and nephews or his friends ever again. How sad he must have felt because you never realize how embedded a person has become in your life until they are no longer around.

As Noah cut each piece of wood and hammered each nail, he couldn't help but think about what was going to happen. Because it took so long to manifest, the people around him thought he was just a crazy old man building a really big boat, but Noah believed what God had said: He was going to destroy the earth and the people in it and start over with Noah's family. That had to be both exhilarating and frightening. Yet, he agreed to do what God had told him to do, and because of that he and his family would be instrumental in God's love mulligan.

God repopulated the earth with Noah and his family, and established the rainbow as a sign of the covenant. Unfortunately, sin crept back into the world and remains to this day.

THE BLUEPRINT

Whenever I prepare to write I always begin with an outline. If I am writing fiction, I work on plot lines and character development in an attempt to create an interesting story. If I am writing non-fiction, I outline what type of book it is going to be and how much research is going to be involved. I

Chapter Fourteen — Don't You Want To Know How I Really Feel?

jot down ideas and thoughts as they come to me (usually in the middle of the night), and I have learned the hard way to always keep paper and pen handy so that I am ready when inspiration strikes. I take the time to write the idea or thought out completely so that when I go back to it I will actually understand what the original intent was. That is something else I have learned the hard way: A great thought in the middle of the night makes no sense in broad daylight if you can't understand what you wrote! I keep all of my notes in a central location until I am ready to begin writing. For me that means waiting for the anointing to write. I know there are authors who write a specific amount of hours each day, but that is not how I work. If I try writing without the anointing, the finished product could best be described as gibberish. However, if I wait until God says, "Write," there is a much better chance that whoever reads my work will be blessed. Once God gives me the go-ahead I pull all of my notes together, and like working on a jigsaw puzzle, I began putting some order to the chaos. During this process I also work out strategic timelines for when certain aspects have to be done to reach my various deadlines.

I think that writing and pregnancy have a lot in common. The seed gets planted from either a sermon or the Scriptures, or something that you have read, heard or observed, and you think, "Wow, that's good. I'm going to use that some day." Then you have the gestation period which is when you fast, pray and research to gather your thoughts about the subject you are going to write about. Then you have the delivery period, which sometimes can go on for a while. One of my friends told me that all three of her children were delivered within fifteen minutes after her water broke. I was in labor five hours (that felt like fifty) with my son. And sometimes labor has to be induced. But either way the baby comes, there is a feeling of elation when you hold him or her in your arms for the first time. That is the same feeling you get when you see something you have created and you realize it really was worth all the effort.

143

DREAMS, PLANS AND GOALS

While listening to my son share the dreams, plans and goals he and his wife have for their children, I realized that this is what God, Jesus and the Holy Spirit did when dreaming and planning for the people of the world. Every parent wants only the best for their children and God is no different. He had been disappointed with Adam and Eve, and gave the world another chance with Noah, only to discover that His people still weren't getting it.

In the beginning God, Jesus and the Holy Spirit agreed on creation. In the end God, Jesus and the Holy Spirit agreed on Jesus' coming to earth as a human. Each had a significant role to play in the process. I can only imagine how the discussion went in heaven when it was decided that Jesus would come to earth. Would He arrive as a grown man, a child or a baby? Would He come to earth performing attention-grabbing signs and wonders, or would He live a low-key life? Would He work alone, or in a group? Would He automatically be accepted as the Messiah, or would there be a struggle for dominance?

Jesus' arrival as a baby wasn't an accident. It had been decided in heaven that He would experience the entire life span of humans to include everything from growing in His mother's womb to taking His last breath on a cross. He would experience the wonder of being held in His mother's arms and rocked to sleep, of learning to crawl and then eventually walking, running and playing in open fields with his friends and family. As He grew older He would learn His earthly father's trade and embrace the satisfaction of creating something with His hands that would last for years to come. Along the way He would whole-heartedly embrace His destiny, and at the appointed time make known His purpose for being in the world.

We usually cannot receive what people are saying unless they can show how they relate to us. At one of the

Chapter Fourteen — Don't You Want To Know How I Really Feel?

meetings of the single parents' ministry a mother was sharing the issues she was experiencing with her children. Other parents were offering her suggestions and she seemed to be receptive to them; however, I noticed that whenever I made a suggestion she shrugged it off. It wasn't until I mentioned my son that her entire posture changed and I realized that up to that point she thought I was just giving her theory and not experience. Once she realized that I was a single parent, too, it made a big difference in her attitude toward what I was saying.

That is the way it is with Jesus; His arrival on earth as an adult would not have had the same affect as His being born a baby. If He had came to earth as an adult then children, teenagers and young adults might not have been able to relate to Him. By coming to earth as a child Jesus experienced the full range of issues that we experience, and He shows us that He is able to both relate to and handle all of our concerns.

Jesus and His Father had discussed what would happen—the good and the bad; the laughter and the tears; the acceptance and rejection—and in spite of that, Jesus entered into full agreement with God that His coming to earth was essential to our well-being.

The plan was to be born of a virgin, live on earth thirty-three years, die a horrible death, ascend to heaven, go back to earth for a set period of time, ascend to heaven again, stay there for an infinite time and then return to earth one final time to reclaim the people He originally came to earth to save.

Jesus gave up a lot so we could have the abundant life because He wants to share with us how He lives. The abundant life isn't just about money; it is about peace of mind, companionship when you are lonely and a spiritual connection to God. The question begs to be asked: If Jesus was willing to give up so much for us, what are you willing to give up for Him?

Obieray Rogers

IMITATION REALLY IS THE SINCEREST
FORM OF FLATTERY

Siblings always like to pick and tease each other and my two grandsons are no different. When the youngest grandson was born, his brother went out of his way to mess with him, but since he was a baby there wasn't much he could do about it. My grandson always gave his brother one of those you-just-wait looks which meant, "You might be bigger than I am now, but once I start walking and talking, I'm going to get you back for messing with me." And that is exactly what happened. Once my youngest grandson realized that he could irritate his brother by mimicking him, he hasn't stopped yanking that particular chain. I always experience a sense of déjà vu when I talk with them on the telephone, because the oldest one talks first and tells me what is new and exciting in his world. Then his brother gets on the phone and repeats word for word what his older brother had just said. Talk about Pete and Re-Pete!

While as humans it is irritating to have someone mimic everything you do, I think that God sometimes wonders why we don't mimic Him. Christians should make everyone they talk to experience a sense of déjà vu, because we should all be saying what God says.

DADDY SAID

I think that grandchildren are the ultimate mulligan because you get a chance to re-do some of the things you wish you had done with your children. I freely admit to being a doting grandmother (as if you haven't already figured that out), but I assure you I balance love with discipline, and between me and their parents we keep them from being spoiled and obnoxious brats. I have shared a lot of anecdotes about my grandchildren throughout this book and you might be tired of hearing about them, but I hope not because they really are very fascinating young people. They

Chapter Fourteen — Don't You Want To Know How I Really Feel?

provide so many teachable moments, so please bear with me as I relate one more story.

My son was a standout basketball player in high school and attended college on a basketball scholarship. After graduation he chose to focus on coaching and personal training as opposed to playing professionally. He is a great coach with a winning record and a sought after personal trainer for high school, college and professional players whose names you see in the newspaper on a regular basis. He loves the game of basketball, and growing up played every day rain or shine, sleet or snow. He has passed his love of the game onto his boys.

One day my youngest grandson was bouncing the basketball with one hand behind his back. When I asked him why he was doing that, he replied, "Daddy said this is how you do it." When he would do something else and I inquired as to why, he would say, "Daddy said this is how you do it." During our conversation, he used the phrase "Daddy said" at least eight times. What I realized was that although he didn't have the first clue about the fundamentals of basketball, he knew someone who did, and he was willing to embrace the concepts, thoughts and actions of what his daddy said to do.

Now my question may be obvious, but I will ask it anyway. If a four-year-old can repeat and then implement what he has heard and seen his daddy do, why can't you? What would happen if you would say yes to God's will for your life? For employment? For health? For happiness? For relationships? Is this a radical concept? Sure. But you know what? God specializes in radical concepts.

Remember the children's game Simon Says? The point of the game was to say or do exactly what Simon said. Why not play an adult version of the game and call it God Says? When God says something, He wants us to say or do exactly what He says. God doesn't tell us things for us to debate them; He tells us things for us to implement them.

Sometimes kids keep asking the same question thinking that the answer is going to change and I know Christians who do the same thing. God's answers never change no matter how many times you ask the question or how cleverly you think you word it. Before you were born God knew all of the not so smart things you would do, the regrets you would have and the disappointments you would face. But as my pastor recently said, "Every day you wake up is an opportunity for a do-over."

Years ago I was the victim of a smear campaign. Rumors were spread about me that were false and just downright mean. What hurt me more than the rumors was the fact that people who should have known better believed what they were hearing. It is interesting that during the entire campaign, not one person came and asked me if it was true. But even if they had, I wouldn't have been able to tell them anything. At the beginning of this vicious campaign God had told me that He would defend me if I would just be quiet. Although I agreed with His plan it was very hard to do. There were times when I wanted to take out a billboard that read, **"I DIDN'T DO ANY OF THE THINGS YOU'RE HEARING!"** but I couldn't. All I could do was ride out the storm.

The rumors eventually were proven to be false, but I still had to endure sly looks and innuendos, and my reputation was sullied, and to this day there are those who still believe what they heard. When it was all said and done, there were some relationships that changed and some that were permanently damaged. You have to be careful who you listen to and hear the meaning behind the words. The devil can and will use anything and anybody so we shouldn't be so quick to embrace the negative. This entire experience taught me a very valuable lesson: God can fight a lot better than I can. As a result of my obedience to God's instructions, He took care of the person who instigated the rumors, as well as those who should have known better than to believe them in the first place.

Chapter Fourteen — Don't You Want To Know How I Really Feel?

My purpose for sharing this story is to point out that some people are more prone to believe a dramatic lie rather than the poignant truth. God has already told you who you are, what you can do, how you will do it and why. Yet, you won't believe Him.

"What more can He say than to you He hath said" is one of the lines in the John Keith song, *How Firm a Foundation.* It is a question I often ask myself when I am struggling with something that God wants me to do that I don't necessarily want to do. How many times does He have to tell you something before you get it? He has already told you that He is trustworthy. All He is waiting on is for you to come into agreement with Him.

Every situation you go through strengthens your faith. That is why it is important to go through situations and not beg God to get you out of them. Coming out on the other side of an experience makes it possible for you to help someone else.

I normally carry a book with me everywhere I go so that I don't sit idly waiting on something or someone. However, that was not the case the day I read the article on agreement that got me interested in learning more about the power behind it. Actually, I was quite frustrated when I got to my doctor's office and realized I didn't have anything to read. While the office always has a variety of current magazines available for patients to peruse, I am usually not interested in whatever is available. Rather than remain frustrated I decided to pick up one of the magazines from the table and it changed my life. As I mentioned in the introduction to this book, I don't remember the name of the magazine or I would have been able to possibly find the author of the article. I will, however, always be grateful for the couple's willingness to share their experience. The family had to go through the birth and death of their son so that years later I would be sitting in my doctor's waiting room reading about what God did for them.

God knew the article would have such an astonishing effect on me that I would never be the same.

God knew I would experience an epiphany regarding the power of agreement sitting in the office.

God knew I would write a book under the anointing of the Holy Spirit entitled *On the Other Side of Yes: Understanding the Power of Agreement.*

God also knew that you would read this and that somehow, some way, you would pass on the information you have learned.

Conclusion

I once attended a conference with some of the women from my church where the speaker had us use one word to describe ourselves, and I chose the word "quiet" at which point everyone burst out laughing. When I asked why, one woman told me, "Obie, you may be a lot of things, but quiet isn't one of them!" I didn't say anything at the time, but later in my hotel room I realized that what caused the laughter was that these women were equating the word "quiet" with the word "shy," and there is a big difference between the two.

I was born the fourth child in a family of six (I have two younger brothers and three older sisters). It was easy to recognize my sisters' unique qualities: my oldest sister is very smart; she made excellent grades throughout her entire matriculation. My second oldest sister is very artistic and creative. My third oldest sister was very dramatic and would have made an outstanding actress. And then there was me.

For as long as I can remember I have always felt like a fish out of water. I have never been good at small talk and could usually be found sitting in a corner reading a book. I remember my mom insisting that I at least speak to people when they came over, which I would do and then return to my space as soon as possible. Meanwhile, my sisters and brothers would be chatting away. To this day I very seldom jump right in and start talking to people I don't know because once I get past hello, how are you? I am pretty much done unless they are going to carry the conversation. However, when I am presenting at a class or a workshop, I become a chameleon and turn "on" because sharing is something I enjoy doing. Besides, who wants to listen to a dull speaker? However, it sometimes surprises people when they see me and I am not "on" because I am by nature an introvert.

I loved school and learning, but I didn't fit in there either. I was too smart for the cool kids and not smart enough for the brainiacs. I was always chosen last for team events. Once I was on the team I tried to do the best I could, but I wasn't athletic so I couldn't contribute much to team sports.

The fish out of water feeling continued into adulthood. A friend of mine had a birthday party and we played some kind of question and answer board game. My team won, but I still remember one of the men from the other team telling me I was too smart and I shouldn't answer so many questions. His criticism hurt because it wasn't as if I was blurting out the answers. My team conferred and then the leader gave the answer. I guess this man figured out that most of the correct answers were being given by me, but what was I supposed to do? Dummy down to make him more comfortable? (Please don't think I am tooting my own horn, because that is not my intention. I just happen to be one of those people who know a little bit about a lot of different things).

I received Christ in my life in 1988 because a friend of mine had gotten saved and I wanted what she had. In 1988 First Church of God in Columbus, Ohio had about a hundred and fifty members, which made it easy to recognize new people. Because most of the people were related to each other (or so it seemed to me at the time), I would have people come up and ask, "Whose family do you belong to?" and my response was to point to my son and say, "His." They then would proceed to give their family's pedigree and its history with First Church. And if you think that once again I felt like a fish out of water, you would be right.

THREE LITTLE WORDS

As a new Christian I tried reading the King James Version of the Bible, but found some of the language challenging. I went to one of the Christian book stores and told them my dilemma. They directed me to a New King James Version which was easier to understand. Someone had told me

Conclusion

about the Living Bible, which is a paraphrase of the Old and New Testament, so I purchased one of those, too. I also purchased a one-year daily devotional and these were the tools I used to study the Bible. I would read the assigned passage in the daily devotional, the New King James and the Living Bible and that is how I learned the Bible. One day a line of Scripture jumped off the page and changed my life forever:

> *You did not choose Me, but I chose you...*
> (John 15:16(a), NKJV)

In 1988 I only absorbed three words from this passage: *I. Chose. You.* Finally, Someone willingly chose me for their team not because the teacher said, "Obie's the only one left," or because one of the team leaders reluctantly said, "I guess I'll take Obie," but because God wanted me.

When I had a child out of wedlock—God chose me.

When I sought to fulfill legitimate needs by illegitimate methods—God chose me.

When every word coming out of my mouth wasn't uplifting—God chose me.

When since salvation I haven't dotted every "I" and crossed every "T"—God chose me.

God chose me, warts and all, because He knows me and loves me anyway. He looked beyond the pretense and chose me!

Those few words of Scripture began to heal the hurts of a little girl who had grown into a woman who had fallen into so many self-destructive traps seeking approval. *I. Chose. You.* Three little words that pack quite a wallop. And you know what? God's choosing isn't like the coupons you clip and never get around to using. There is no expiration date. God's choosing is forever, and it is final!

"He chose us in Him before the foundation of the world" (Ephesians 1:4). Before He created the world, God had already planned on the creation of man, and God knew

153

I would be born on March 30, 1954 and re-born on December 22, 1988, when I accepted Him into my life. Since that time, God has demonstrated what He meant what He said "I chose you":

- <u>I am never alone</u>: *"I have been with you wherever you have gone and I have destroyed all of your enemies"* (2 Samuel 7:9(a), NLT).

- <u>God has big plans for me if I will just believe him</u>: *"Abraham never wavered in believing God's promises. In fact, his faith grew stronger, and in this he brought glory to God. He was absolutely convinced that God was able to do anything He promised"* (Romans 4:20-21, NLT).

- <u>God is going to save my family</u>: *"Fear not, for I am with you; I will bring your descendants from the east, and gather you from the west; I will say to the north, 'Give them up!' And to the south, 'Do not keep them back!' Bring My sons from afar, and My daughters from the ends of the earth* (Isaiah 43:5-6, NKJV).

- <u>I don't have to be afraid</u>: *"For I, the Lord your God, will hold your right hand, Saying to you, 'Fear not, I will help you'"* (Isaiah 41:13, NKJV).

- <u>I am constantly on God's mind</u>: *"Can a mother forget her nursing child? Can she feel no love for a child she has borne? But even if that were possible, I would not forget you! See, I have written your name on my hand"* (Isaiah 49:15-16, NLT).

- <u>I don't have to worry about anything</u>: *"I am leaving you with a gift—peace of mind and heart. And the peace I give isn't like the peace the world gives. So don't be troubled or afraid"* (John 14:27, NLT).

Conclusion

- <u>God always keeps His Word</u>: *"What's more, I am with you, and I will protect you wherever you go. One day I will bring you back to this land. I will not leave you until I have finished giving you everything I have promised you"* (Genesis 28:15, NLT).

- <u>God has promised to be with me forever</u>: *"...Never will I leave you; never will I forsake you"* (Hebrews 13:5, NIV).

It would be several years later that I fully embraced the entirety of John 15:16:

> *"You did not choose Me, but I chose you and appointed you that you should go and bear fruit, and that your fruit should remain, that whatever you ask the Father in My name He may give you."*

I realize that my "fruit to remain" is words. Every class I have ever taught, every workshop I have ever conducted, every word I have ever written are all evidence of my fruit. My words will still have an affect long after I have written and spoken them. The childhood rhyme: "Sticks and stones may break my bones, but words will never hurt me," isn't true. Words can hurt, and we have to be careful how we use them. Words have so much power that God used them to speak the world into existence.

THE QUANTRY OF BEING CHOSEN

The first choosing God does is when He woos you to come to Him. Once you say yes, God is then in a position to give you a specific assignment, one that only you can accomplish. The unique abilities that God has given you will reach a specific group of people, even if other people are doing a similar work. For example, you may be called to preach or teach and although there are other preachers and teachers, God may want to use your particular style to reach a specific group of people. Should you choose to accept the assignment, it is then your responsibility to stay in your lane of anointing. In other words, don't try to be a poor imitation of someone else. You are an original so act like it! In a ministers' class taught by my pastor, one of the male preachers asked what you were to do when a church invites you to speak and they expect you to do an imitation of Bishop Clarke. Bishop's response was that you had to be yourself, because there were people looking for your voice, your style, your gift.

Ask God to show you what He wants you to do. Every Christian has been given at least one gift and one talent, and it is our responsibility to determine what it is and how we are to use what God has given us. And we must keep in mind that God chooses us for the way we will become, not necessarily the way we are now. Once God reveals your assignment, stay true to yourself. If God has chosen you to do something for Him, you need to be about the business of bringing whatever that is forth.

When God puts His hand on your life, He will begin to show you mind-boggling things. You may have a tendency to share with those you normally share with, but be careful. Everybody is not going to be able to receive what God has shown you, what God has said to you or where God is leading you. People mean well, but they can only advise you based on their own experiences, and their experience is not going to be the same as your experience. You need to find someone who has been where God is taking you.

Mary and Elizabeth are excellent examples of this. Both women were pregnant at the same time and would deliver male children within months of each other. Both pregnancies were highly anticipated, but totally unexpected. And neither woman had anyone they could honestly talk to about what they were experiencing. If Sarah were still alive,

Conclusion

Elizabeth would have been able to at least talk with someone who got pregnant long past the childbearing years; unfortunately Sarah had been deceased for decades when Elizabeth was pregnant. But for Mary, there was no one who had ever been in her position. However, Mary knew that at least Elizabeth would under-stand about miraculous conceptions, so she went to visit her. The Bible says that, *"At the sound of Mary's greeting, Elizabeth's child leaped within her, and Elizabeth was filled with the Holy Spirit"* (Luke 2:41, NLT). You need to only share with those who can make the baby inside of you leap. The baby inside of you if whatever assignment you have been given by God. You are to nurture it and watch over it and at the appointed time bring it forth.

SOMETIMES IT REALLY IS ALL ABOUT YOU

One of the concepts parents try to teach their children is to share, which is a good trait to learn, but I personally think its okay to be selfish sometimes. That doesn't mean that you won't share or that you don't know how to share. It just means that whatever you have is so good that you want to keep it to yourself, at least for a little while.

I have a nice house, but there are people who have nicer homes. I have a good job, but there are people with better jobs. I have gifts and talents, but there are people who possess more gifts and talents than I. While I may not have a lot of things, one thing I do have is Jesus. There is none greater. There is none better. There is none equal.

There are a lot of hymns that hold special meaning to me, but throughout the writing of this chapter, there was one song title that consistently came to my mind: *Blessed Assurance, Jesus is Mine!* (Words and music by Fannie Crosby and Phoebe P. Knapp).

Jesus is mine. I can keep Him to myself or I can share Him, and He will still be mine. I can rely on Him, and He will still be mine. I can tell Him everything and anything and He will still be my friend. He is not going to use what I have told Him against me. He doesn't hold grudges. He doesn't compare me to anyone else. He doesn't expect me to be a poor imitation of another person. He expects me to be me, and helps me be the best me I can be.

But, this is what I want you to remember, blessed assurance Jesus is mine can only be true if you choose Him in return.

CHOOSING WORKS BOTH WAYS

You can choose paint colors, clothes, cars and friends. You can choose which restaurant to go to or where you want to live or work. You can choose which church you will attend and where you will vacation. So why not choose Jesus?

If you haven't, you will never live your life to its fullest. You will always be searching for something you will never find. You will never know who you can trust or who will have your back during a crisis. So why not choose Jesus?

I experienced the first heartbreak of love in the fourth grade. Yep, I learned early! A boy that I liked asked me if I liked him in return. I said yes and he considered us boyfriend and girlfriend. Unfortunately, the love affair was short-lived. By recess he had already chosen a new girlfriend. Oh, well. Nothing lasts forever, right? Wrong.

That boy asked me a simple question: I like you, do you like me? God is asking the same question: I like you—and I have proven it in so many ways—do you like me back? He is waiting on an answer.

Some people play on other's emotions and feelings, but for the most part I think that when someone promises to love you forever, they mean it at the time. But, because we are human, things happen and feelings change. The only One who can promise anything forever is God:

Conclusion

I know that whatever God does, it shall be forever. Nothing can be added to it, and nothing can be taken from it (Ecclesiastes 3:14(a)).

God taps us on the shoulder and says, "I choose you." We then have a choice: Do we ignore what God is trying to do in our lives, or do we choose Him back. The reward for choosing God is so much greater than the obstacles. Even when things get crazy in your life—and they will, because being saved doesn't exempt you from life's traumas and dramas—you will have Someone who will take you through the challenges. Jesus is well able to handle whatever issues come your way.

If you have never invited Jesus into your life, now would be the perfect time. Saying yes to God makes you part of the greatest agreement you will ever make. Just say this simple prayer out loud:

Father, please forgive me for all the times I have tried to do things my way instead of yours. I confess that I am a sinner and I cannot save myself. I believe that Jesus Christ is your Son who died on the cross in my place. I believe that He rose on the third day and ascended into heaven, where He sits at your right hand. I believe that He is coming back again. Please come into my heart and cleanse me from all sin and unrighteousness. Please fill me with the precious Holy Spirit. From this day forward I belong to you, and I accept you as my Lord and Savior. In Jesus' name. Amen.

Once you have prayed this, you are saved. Don't worry if you don't "feel" saved. The Bible says, *"For if you confess with your mouth that Jesus is Lord and believe in your heart that God raised him from the dead, you will be saved"* (Romans 10:9, NLT). After you have prayed, there are three things you need to do:

First, find a church where the Bible is being taught and preached. There is a church on just about every corner, and you may have to visit a few before you find the right one. But, whatever you do don't neglect getting together with brothers and sisters of a like mind.

Second, find a Bible that you can read and understand. Ask your friends for a recommendation or go to a Christian bookstore and ask them for suggestions. Examine several versions until you find one that is appropriate for where you are right now. You may change to another version as you spiritually mature, but it is important that you not neglect this aspect of your spiritual education. Don't focus on memorizing the entire Bible or even trying to read the entire Bible right away. Take it slow. A good place to start is with the Gospels: Matthew, Mark, Luke and John, and the Psalms. As you become more comfortable with the Word, you will branch out to other books of the Bible.

Third, tell everybody you meet what the Lord has done for you. No one can tell your story like you can. Don't worry about what to say; just tell the truth in your own words. And make sure you e-mail me at obierogers@aol.com so I can rejoice with you.

May the Lord bless and protect you.
May the Lord smile on you and be gracious to you.
And may the Lord show you His favor and
give you His peace.
Numbers 6:24-26, NLT

Questions for Reflection and Discussion

1.   How do you respond when asked to do a favor?
    a.   Impulsively—"Sure, no problem."
    b.   Cautiously—"Uh, I'm not sure."
    c.   Wisely—"Tell me what you need and I will let you know if I can do it or not."

2.   Can you think of a time you agreed to do something and then regretted saying yes?
    a.   How did you handle the situation?
    b.   Did you learn anything from the experience?

3.   Can you think of a time God wanted you to pave the way for someone else by going first?
    a.   If you were obedient, what were the results?
    b.   If you were reluctant to step out in faith, what prevented you from obeying the Lord?

4.   How do you feel when something you do doesn't get acknowledged?
    a.   Is there anything you can do about it?
    b.   Are you more conscious about showing appreciation to others?

5.   Have you ever been the victim of deception?
    a.   How did it make you feel?
    b.   What have you done to make sure it doesn't happen again?
    c.   Is all deception wrong?

6. Can you think of at least one time where God did something so awesome that all you could say was, "Wow!"?

    a. What did you do in response to what had happened?

    b. Did the experience draw you closer to God?

7. How is your prayer life?

    a. Do you think that God can only move in one way?

    b. How many different ways have you seen God move in your life?

8. Have you ever received a surprise from God?

    a. How did it make you feel?

    b. Did it change your perception of surprises?

9. Have you ever unknowingly participated in something that hurt someone else?

    a. What did you do about it?

    b. What steps did you take to make sure it didn't happen again?

10. Have you ever done something so senseless that all you could do was shake your head?

    a. What, if any, were the consequences of your actions?

    b. Did you realize that God had covered you?

11. Do you know God's will for your life?

    a. If yes, are you walking in God's will?

    b. If you do not know God's will for your life, have you asked God to reveal His will to you?

12. What is your definition of faith? I know what the Bible says, but what do you think it is?
    a. Is there such a thing as negative faith?
    b. Why or why not?

13. Are you doing what God has asked you to do?
    a. If you are, how do you feel?
    b. If you are not, what is the challenge to obeying God?

14. Are you emulating God by saying what He says?
    a. In what way are you imitating God?
    b. What do you do when you miss the mark?

15. Is the way you handle hurt and disappointment now the same way you handled hurt and disappointment in the past?

16. Have you discovered that with each new experience—whether good or bad—God gives you new insight and strength for what you are going through?

Other Books by Obieray Rogers

Waiting for Boaz: Encouragement for women desiring marriage God's way — ISBN 978-0-9764022-1-3

Most people will agree that relationships take work, regardless of whether it is between friends, family or a potential romantic partner. All relationships require prayer, guidance and patience, especially if you are talking about marriage. There is a big difference between a good marriage and a great marriage, and a big part of the difference is choosing the right mate. God has provided a blueprint for the ideal mate for His women in Boaz, that Old Testament prototype of Jesus Christ. Unfortunately, many women would say they ended up with Bozo instead because they chose to step out ahead of God. Why does this happen? How does this happen? Well, to find the answers you will have to read the book!

The Heaven on Earth Trilogy (fiction)

Book One—*A Hug From Daddy*
ISBN 978-0-9764022-2-0

Book Two—*The Wonder of Love*
ISBN 978-14495628-9-2

Book Three—*Kiss Yesterday Goodbye*
ISBN 978-14664224-1-4
Available January 2012

WWW.OBIEROGERS.COM
A fresh voice in Christian fiction and inspiration.